STEPPING STONES TO FURTHER
JEWISH-CHRISTIAN RELATIONS

An unabridged collection of
Christian Documents

STEPPING STONES TO FURTHER JEWISH-CHRISTIAN RELATIONS

Foreword by

Edward A Synan

Compiled by

Helga Croner

STIMULUS BOOKS
LONDON NEW YORK

Volume I. Studies in Judaism and Christianity

First published in 1977

ISBN 0905967 00 3
© *Stimulus Books*

Published by Stimulus Books, London and New York,
Printed in England by Dorling Print Group Ltd., London SW20 0LN

To
BARBARA and MARGRIT
Christopher, Melanie, Karen, Jennifer

TABLE OF CONTENTS

d) LATIN AMERICAN STATEMENTS (JOINT JEWISH-CHRISTIAN)

II. Protestant Documents

a) STATEMENTS BY THE WORLD COUNCIL OF CHURCHES

b) STATEMENTS BY VARIOUS CHURCH GROUPS

III. Joint Protestant-Catholic Document

FOREWORD

After mutual recrimination that has lasted too long between the Jewish People and those who see in Jesus of Nazareth both the hope of Israel and the light given to the Gentiles, our time is experiencing a reversal of attitudes. Welcome though this change must be, it entails yet another peril. In our anxiety to strike out in a new direction, to be "ecumenical" and pacific, we might be tempted to gloss over real dissent and to ignore misgivings on either side. No matter how well-intentioned, a development of this stripe would be a disaster; through it our new-found goodwill would dissipate in a rhetorical vapor. Far from establishing peace, we should earn the Prophets' strictures against crying "Peace!" where there is no peace (Ezek 13:10) or, under an appearance of peace, devouring the people (Mic 3:5).

One strength of this collection of Christian texts is that awkward questions are raised with a candor that can only honor both Jew and Christian. No defense is proffered for those long centuries during which Christian concern for God's Chosen was notable by its absence, nor for the appalling injustices against the Jews, and still less for the deficient theological constructions by which those crimes were rationalized. More than once Christian unease in our days over displaced Islamic populations has been set out in these pages and the ambiguities inseparable from any state have been acknowledged to be a special burden for the State of Israel. Is it an instance of a "double standard" when modern Israel is held to a more exacting ethico-political norm than are other nations, given that her claim to exist appeals beyond the labor and sufferings of her founders to the Promise? A Synod of the Dutch Reformed Church raises a whole series of misgivings that, in the eyes of many, afflict the origin and the history of Israel. Is this "exemplary" State not "human, all too human"? Were not the entries into the Land under Joshua and Nehemia morally speaking "dubious affairs"? Is it not the case that non-Jews now are treated by Israel as second class citizens?

Having drawn attention to these evidences of reserve, a commentator is bound to note as well that this Reformed Church body seems to assume the conversion of the Jewish People to Christianity in the Last Time and this in a way hardly more nuanced than was the case with Christian jurists and theologians of the middle ages. A happier formulation, in a document that occurs earlier in this volume, has it that fidelity to the Covenant between the Jews and their Lord was linked to the gift of the Land and that this implies no judgment on historical occurrences, no decisions of a purely political order.

Statements from the Roman Catholic community in the United States fulfill the banal expectation that cis-atlantic interventions will tend to be "practical," even "pragmatic," whereas those from Europe are likely to be irredeemably "speculative." On the other hand, if Catholic voices from the United States raise the practical difficulty of state aid to non-public schools and often descend to the details of dialogue on various levels, they have not failed to note that the negative side of what Paul of Tarsus wrote on Judaism has been so adequately handled that today we might well explore the more positive elements in his teaching on the Jewish People.

In this connection a Lutheran document, remarking that the theological paradox which confronted Luther when he tried to unravel the enigma of the Jews "was too much for him," is a felicitous combination of reverence for the man who gave form to their tradition with a confession that he failed to reconcile his allegiançe to Jesus with the providential role of the community from which Jesus has come to Christians.

Over the whole volume presides the rubric, repeatedly expressed, that Jews must be understood as they understand themselves, that Christians must be seen by Jews as Christians define themselves. This is the condition without which nothing can be hoped; both sides have age-old misconceptions precisely because traditionally each has seen the other from the outside. For a Christian to see a Jew as "the other" is already to misunderstand the Christian heritage; less obvious, perhaps, but defensible nonetheless, is the assertion that a Jew cannot perceive the Christian as "the other" without diminishing the fecundity of Prophet and Psalmist. Above all, and this volume makes the point in a text from a Commission of the World Council of Churches, there can be no proselytizing in the "derogatory sense," no "cajolery, undue pressure, or intimidation." '

When Pope John XXIII quoted Cardinal Newman (for the first time in a papal document, his own first Encyclical *Ad Petri Cathedram*) this was hailed as evidence of newly opened windows; how much more striking that a Roman pronouncement from the pontificate of Paul VI should cite the great Protestant theologian Karl Barth! As always, Barth had produced a memorable saying: ". . . the ecumenical movement is driven by the Spirit of the Lord. But do not forget, there is only one really important question: Our relations with Israel." Is not the brute fact that a Protestant theologian has been quoted by a commission of Roman Catholic bishops as memorable as what Barth has said? Here the mystery of Israel has borne the unlooked-for fruit of one more small step toward healing the sixteenth century rift within Christendom.

Logicians are fond of reminding us that words are more than carriers of meaning. Words are facts, things in the world, and in this perspective words are not merely signs of things other than themselves. Indeed, one use of language that beguiles contemporaries of ours who have a philosophical bent is "performative." The saying of some words in some circumstances can be the doing of a deed. To pronounce the words "I do" in an appropriate situation constitutes a performance that *is* a marriage.

Seldom can a collection of documents have verified so dramatically as does this book the twofold nature of human words. All of it, the whole complex of sentences, terms, and paragraphs, has meaning to be sure; still, this book may well be more important when it is taken simply as a fact in the world, as an event, as a performance. To write certain of its sentences has been to perform an act of friendship or an act of contrition, even to fulfill a demand of justice. That so many and such diverse Christian voices have spoken in these ways can be more important than the detail of what they have said. We may not have heard a friend clearly enough to understand what he has said, but the fact that he has spoken at all is enough to assure us that a darkened room is not empty.

For two millennia, as one document in this volume recalls, dialogue was generally impossible. Put another way, the darkened room seemed empty of friends, for seldom was the silence broken by a friendly voice and frequently the silence was rent by accusations, by propaganda, by conflict. To change the image to that of this volume's title, some of the stones may be slippery, some perhaps ought to be re-located, but stepping-stones are in place. On them we dare hope to cross, for Jews must know that they have friends on the other side.

Edward A. Synan,

Priest of the Archdiocese of Newark, N.J.

President, The Pontifical Institute of Mediaeval Studies, Toronto, Ont.

ACKNOWLEDGMENTS

Grateful acknowledgment is made to the following organizations for making material available to me: U.S. Bishops' Secretariat for Jewish-Christian Relations, Washington, D.C.; SIDIC, Rome; Episcopal Catechetical Institute and Episcopal Vicar of Vienna, Austria; Anti-Defamation League of B'nai B'rith, New York; World Council of Churches, Geneva; National Council of the Churches of Christ in the U.S.A., New York; Freiburger Rundbrief, Freiburg, Germany; Gütersloher Verlagshaus Gerd Mohn, Germany. My personal gratitude is extended to Dr. Franz von Hammerstein, Geneva; Dr. William Weiler, New York; Rabbi Leon Klenicki, New York; Prof. Luc Dequeker, Louvain; Dr. Michael Brocke, Regensburg. They drew my attention to various publications and thereby helped me to make this collection as complete as possible.

Responsibility for the unwitting omission of any document as well as for the translation of papers originally published in a foreign language—unless otherwise noted—is mine alone.

Since this is document material, no attempt was made to unify style, spelling, capitalization, etc.

Helga Croner

I. ROMAN CATHOLIC DOCUMENTS

(a) STATEMENTS BY VATICAN AUTHORITIES

Vatican II on the Jews. **Nostra Aetate** *(n. 4), October 1965. This conciliar Statement is part of the Declaration on the Relationship of the Church to Non-Christian Religions.*

As this Sacred Synod searches into the mystery of the Church, it remembers the bond that spiritually ties the people of the New Covenant to Abraham's stock.

Thus the Church of Christ acknowledges that, according to God's saving design, the beginnings of her faith and her election are found already among the Patriachs, Moses and the prophets. She professes that all who believe in Christ — Abraham's sons according to faith — are included in the same Patriarch's call, and likewise that the salvation of the Church is mysteriously foreshadowed by the chosen people's exodus from the land of bondage. The Church, therefore, cannot forget that she received the revelation of the Old Testament through the people with whom God in His inexpressible mercy concluded the Ancient Covenant. Nor can she forget that she draws sustenance from the root of that well-cultivated olive tree onto which has been grafted the wild shoot, the Gentiles. Indeed, the Church believes that by His cross Christ Our Peace reconciled Jews and Gentiles, making both one in Himself.

The Church keeps ever in mind the words of the Apostle about his kinsmen: "Theirs is the sonship and the glory and the covenants and the law and the worship and the promises; theirs are the fathers and from them is the Christ according to the flesh" (Rom 9:4-5), the Son of the Virgin Mary. She also recalls that the Apostles, the Church's mainstay and pillars, as well as most of the early disciples who proclaimed Christ's Gospel to the world, sprang from the Jewish people.

As Holy Scripture testifies, Jerusalem did not recognize the time of her visitation, nor did the Jews, in large number, accept the Gospel; indeed not a few opposed its spreading. Nevertheless God holds the Jews most dear for the sake of their Fathers; He does not repent of the gifts He makes or of the calls He issues — such is the witness of the Apostle. In company with the Prophets and the same Apostle, the Church awaits that day, known to God alone, on which all peoples will address the Lord in a single voice and "serve him shoulder to shoulder" (Soph 3:9).

Since the spiritual patrimony common to Christians and Jews is thus so great, this Sacred Synod wants to foster and recommend that mutual understanding and respect which is the fruit, above all, of biblical and theological studies as well as of fraternal dialogues.

True, the Jewish authorities and those who followed their lead pressed for the death of Christ; still, what happened in His passion cannot be charged against all the Jews, without distinction, then alive, nor against the Jews of today. Although the Church is the new people of God, the Jews should not be presented as rejected or accursed by God, as if this followed from the Holy Scriptures. All should see to it, then, that in catechetical work or in the preaching of the word of God they do not teach anything that does not conform to the truth of the Gospel and the spirit of Christ.

Furthermore, in her rejection of every persecution against any man, the Church, mindful of the patrimony she shares with the Jews and moved not by political reasons but by the Gospel's spiritual love, decries hatred, persecutions, displays of anti-Semitism, directed against Jews at any time and by anyone.

Besides, as the Church has always held and holds now, Christ underwent His passion and death freely, because of the sins of men and out of infinite love, in order that all may reach salvation. It is, therefore, the burden of the Church's preaching to proclaim the cross of Christ as the sign of God's all-embracing love and as the fountain from which every grace flows.

Introduction to the discussions of the Plenary Session of bishop members of the Secretariat for Promoting Christian Unity, which demonstrates the spirit in which the work at an official level of the Church was carried out. Rome, November 1969.
(Quoted from Information Service No. 9, February 1970/1, of the Secretariat for Promoting Christian Unity)

I. It is in "searching into the mystery of the Church" itself *(Nostra Aetate)* that the Council was led to recall the bond that unites the Christian people to the descendants of Abraham. The Declaration published on that occasion, is a document that inaugurates a new era in the relations of Christians and Jews. The heritage of the past, it is true, still weighs heavily on these relations. But in the light of the clear affirmations of the Council, all Christians are called to an effort of comprehension and searching, which ought to translate itself into action in order that this document should not remain a dead letter. With a view to promoting this research and its application the following reflections and suggestions are proposed.

II. After four years it is possible to take stock of our situation. Four attitudes can be set out with respect to the problem of the Jewish-Christian relations:

(*a*) That of those who have recognized that Christianity cannot be understood in its origin and its very nature without reference to the Jewish tradition wherein it took root and which is still very much alive in our own day.

(*b*) That of the "indifferent" who do not see how this problem can affect their situation as Christians (either because Judaism in itself presents no problem to them, or because *de facto* there are no Jews in the region in which they live).

(*c*) That of those who, not only forget "the patrimony they have in common with Jews" *(Nostra Aetate),* but who are still motivated by a more or less conscious or declared anti-Semitism, all manifestations of which the council has deplored *(Nostra Aetate,* n. 4).

(*d*) That of those who, often by ignorance, exaggerating or generalizing from individual cases, consider the Jewish people of our day as almost totally "secularized", even atheist, and therefore without any further religious significance.

III. In order to further the concrete application of the Declaration *Nostra Aetate,* n. 4, and in the spirit that inspires it, it appears useful to us to recall the following:

(*a*) The problem of the relations between Jews and Christians concerns the *Church as such,* since it is in "searching into its own mystery" that it comes upon the mystery of Israel. These relations touch therefore upon the Christian conscience and Christian life in all its aspects (liturgy, catechesis, preaching, etc.) in all countries where the Church is established, and not only where it is in contact with Jews.

(*b*) The New Testament itself affirms the permanent value of the *Sacred Books* on which the faith of the Jewish people is founded and from which it is nourished. "Think not that I have come to abolish the law and the Prophets; I have come not to abolish them but to fulfill them" (Mt 5:17); "to them belong the sonship, the glory, the covenants, the giving of the law, the worship and the promises; to them belong the patriarchs . . ." (Rom 9:4); the Jews "are beloved for the sake of their forefathers. For the gifts and the call of God are irrevocable" (Rom 11:28-29).

(*c*) The Church is not born solely of scripture but also of the living tradition of the Jewish people. Providence has not limited itself to a "simple bookish preparation of the coming of the Messiah" (L. Bouyer, *La Bible et l'Evangile,* 2, 248). Christ, His apostles, and the first Christians participated in this tradition. "As transforming as Christian revelation may be, it is from the Jewish tradition that it draws not only its formulas, its images, its setting, but even the marrow of its concepts" (*ibid.* 250). Christianity, on the other hand, is not bound directly to the Old Testament as such, but rather as it was interpreted by the ancient Jewish tradition.

Recent research by exegetes and liturgists has come to the conclusion that in order fully to understand Christian tradition and institutions it is *indispensable* to examine Jewish institutions themselves in depth. This is particularly clear in the case of the origin of the sacraments, Christians have adopted the Jewish feasts and prayers, adapting them to the Revelation brought by Christ. Their fundamental meaning, however, can be grasped only by constant reference to the original milieu. But the Jewish liturgy is still celebrated today in the same terms as in the ancient period when the first Christians participated in it. What more suggestive way is there to understand the institution of the Eucharist in the setting of the Jewish Passover meal than the Passover *Seder* in a Jewish family!

(*d*) This same fact has been confirmed on the plane of theological research. Every exploration of the fundamental notions of the Christian religion leads to a confrontation with analogous doctrines of inter-testamental Judaism into which they find a point of insertion. It was Providence itself which willed that the Revelation of Christ find its starting point in the doctrines we see circulating in Palestinian Judaism of the first century.

The eschatological and apocalyptical conceptions of sin and redemption, the Incarnation as a presence of the Word of God among us, and other themes again—all this cannot be studied without a profound familiarity with the world of Jewish tradition, not alone of the time of Christ, but as it was formulated at all stages and in every form of Jewish literature as well.

Let us raise two points as examples, in which Christian theology can only be enriched by contact with the Jewish religious tradition.

(*aa*) The concept of *salvation history*. In the Bible we observe that God reveals Himself concretely in events, in relations with real men: YHWH is the God of someone, of "Abraham of Isaac and of Jacob." God saves by acting. No fact or event eludes the design of "God the Saviour."

Thus has the Jewish religion always conceived its relations with God.

How then, in the Christian view, can we understand what "salvation history" means, that Revelation of God in and by history, without taking into consideration the manner in which the chosen people became aware of the encounter with God and lived this Revelation of a God ever present throughout its long history down to the present time?

(*bb*) *The conception of the world.* All believers, Jewish and Christian have confronted the world of the "death of God," of *secularization,* or by whatever name one describes this placing of God in parentheses or excluding Him from His creation. Well, in face of this contemporary problem, the Jewish conception of the world as a permanent creation of God, of the living conception of the action and presence of the Creator in all His works—such a conception can help us to remain faithful to the biblical sense of a sort of "consecration" of the universe.

Here are some examples, of which there are more, which could likewise illustrate the contribution that Jewish tradition makes to Christian theology when the latter returns to the sources common to Jews and Christians.

IV. Since the problem of relations with Jews is tied to the very mystery of the Church (*Nostra Aetate*), all Christian Churches are *de facto* involved in the problem. It has therefore an *ecumenical* aspect which it is important to emphasize in the context with which we are dealing. The Christian Churches are divided and we are seeking the unity willed by the Lord. This unity cannot be built except by a return to the common sources, to the origins of faith.

Experience shows, in fact, that whenever the dialogue between Jews and Christians has developed, ecumenical dialogue has itself gained in depth and vitality. When Pope Paul VI addressed the participants of the Congress of International Organizations for the Study of the Old Testament, which brought together Jewish, Protestant, and Catholic scholars, he declared in an audience of April 19, 1968: "The three families, Jewish, Protestant, and Catholic equally hold it (Old Testament) in honor. They are therefore able to study and venerate these Sacred Books together . . . It is fortunate that the initiative of this joint study has been taken . . . This is an authentic and fruitful form of ecumenical work indeed" (*L'Osservatore Romano,* April 20, 1968). The deepening of ecumenical relations leads necessarily to an encounter with the Jewish people. K. Barth remarked in 1966: "There are now many good contacts between the Catholic Church and many Protestant Churches, between the Secretariat of Christian Unity and the World Council of Churches. The ecumenical movement is driven by the Spirit of the Lord. But do not forget, there is only one really important question: our relations with Israel."

Many bishops have seen this connection and have established commissions for Jewish-Christian relations in the framework of agencies in charge of ecumenical questions. This ecumenical context shows the spirit in which Jewish-Christian relations should be established and developed.

This spirit can be called ecumenical insofar as the term expresses concern to know the other as he is and as he defines himself; concern to love and respect him in his convictions and in the conceptions which rule his life.

Reflections and Suggestions for the Application of the Directives of
Nostra Aetate *(n. 4). Working Document prepared for the Holy See's*
Office for Catholic-Jewish Relations, by a special Commission.
December 1969.
(Quoted from Documentary Service, *December 16, 1969, of the Press*
Department, U.S. Catholic Conference)

Introduction

At the present time the Church is attentive to those new tasks which a world in the throes of rapid cultural, social, and religious changes has thrust upon her. Vatican Council II *(Gaudium et Spes),* is cognizant of the fresh aspirations of humanity that seek to preserve the liberty and dignity of the human person and still other human values in a period of transition and searching. It is against such a background that the new encounter between the Church and Judaism is taking place.

The Declaration of Vatican Council II on Non-Christian Religions of 1965 marks an important turning point in the history of Jewish-Catholic relations. It is a considerable step forward. After two millenia, generally characterized by mutual ignorance and frequent conflict, it has presented the opportunity to engage in or pursue a dialogue aimed at better mutual understanding. In the last four years in various countries numerous initiatives have been taken in this direction, and it has been possible to ascertain better the conditions of this new relationship. The moment is apparently here to gauge with precision the directions the Council has taken and, as a fruit of the experience gained, to offer concrete suggestions that will truly help to achieve the aims of the conciliar document in the life of the Church.

Cognizance is increasingly being gained in the Church of the actual place of the Jewish people in the history of salvation and of its permanent election. This fact points toward a theological renewal and toward a new Christian reflection on the Jewish people that it is important to pursue. On the other hand, it appears that still too often Christians do not know what Jews are. They do not, in any case, see them as they are in themselves and as they define themselves in their present and living reality, as the people of the Bible living in our midst. They do not see them as that people which in its history has encountered the living and true God, the One God who established with that people a covenant, of which circumcision is the sign, the God who accomplished in its favor a miraculous Exodus, which it relives each year in its Passover, both as a remembrance of its past and an expectation of the full realization of its promises. This same God has revealed Himself to His people Israel and made to it the gift of the Torah.

And He has confided to it a word that "endures forever" (Is 40:8), a word that has become an unquenchable source of life and prayer, in a tradition that has not ceased to enrich itself through the centuries.

Fidelity to the covenant was linked to the gift of a land, which in the Jewish soul has endured as the object of an aspiration that Christians should strive to understand. In the wake of long generations of painful exile, all too often aggravated by persecutions and moral pressures, for which Christians ask pardon of their Jewish brothers, Jews have indicated in a thousand ways their attachment to the land promised to their ancestors from the days of Abraham's calling. It could seem that Christians, whatever the difficulties they may experience, must attempt to understand and respect the religious significance of this link between the people and the land. The existence of the State of Israel should not be separated from this perspective; which does not in itself imply any judgment on historical occurrences or on decisions of a purely political order.

But if such mutual comprehension is indispensable for dialogue between Christians and Jews, reflection on the mystery of Israel is also indispensable for Christianity to define itself, both as to its origins and in its nature as people of God. Without question, many elements from diverse civilizations have ultimately contributed to making Christianity what it is in its doctrines and its institutions; it is no less true that it was within Judaism that Christianity was born and wherein it found essential elements of its faith and cult. From the experience lived in the covenant with God emerged the Christian universe, which derived from that experience the very marrow of its concepts.

The dignity of the human person requires the condemnation of all forms of anti-Semitism *(Nostra Aetate)*. In view of these relations of the Church and the Jewish people, it is easier to see how anti-Semitism is essentially opposed to the spirit of Christianity. Still more do these relations show forth the duty of better understanding and mutual esteem.

In keeping with these considerations, we propose a few suggestions that will apply to the principal areas of the life of the Church as well as to relations with Jews.

Dialogue

Relations between Christians and Jews have for the most part been no more than a monologue. A true dialogue must now be established. The dialogue, in effect, comprises a favored means for promoting better mutual understanding and a deepening of one's own tradition. The condition of dialogue is respect for the other as he is, for his faith and religious convictions. All intent of proselytizing and conversion is excluded. Great openness of mind, distrust of one's own prejudices, and tact, such are the indispensable qualities required if one is not, even unconsciously, to offend the other party to the dialogue. In addition to fraternal conversations and biblical studies in common, meetings of competent persons to study problems that may arise are to be fostered.

Whenever possible and mutually desirable, meeting before God in prayer and silent meditation should be encouraged. This practice can create that openness of spirit and humility of heart so necessary for understanding of self and others. It is indicated in particular when dealing with major questions, such as those of justice and peace.

Liturgy

We call to mind the strong link that binds Christian liturgy to the Jewish one, which continues to live in our own time. The fundamental conception of liturgy as expression of community life conceived as service of God and mankind is common to Jews and Christians. We grasp the importance for Jewish-Christian relations of an awareness of these common forms of prayer (texts, feasts, rites, etc.) in which the Bible holds an essential place.

An effort must be made to understand better that the Old Testament retains its proper validity *(Dei Verbum)*. This should not be denied by reason of the subsequent interpretation of the New Testament. The Old Testament should not be understood exclusively in reference to the New, nor reduced to an allegorical significance, as is so often done in the Christian liturgy.

In biblical textual commentaries, without overlooking the points of separation, the continuity of our faith with that of the Old Covenant should be underscored, particularly from the point of view of the promises and the common expectation of their eschatological fulfillment.

With respect to Bible readings, much care should be taken in the homily with respect to right interpretations, especially of those texts which seem to put the Jewish people in an unfavorable light. Meanwhile, the faithful should be instructed in such a manner that they will understand all texts in their true sense and in the meaning these should have for the believer of today.

Commissions in charge of liturgical translations must be particularly attentive to the manner of presenting expressions or passages which can be interpreted in a tendentious fashion by uninformed Christians. Thus, the phrase "the Jews" in St. John can at times be translated according to context, by "the leaders of the Jews" or the "enemies of Jesus," expressions which give a better rendering of the thought of the Evangelist and avoid the appearance of involving the Jewish people as such. Another example is that of the words "Pharisee" and "Pharisaism," which have acquired an especially pejorative coloring. Reference should be made here to exegetical studies.

The foregoing remarks apply as well to introductions to biblical readings, to the *Oratio fidelium,* and to commentaries in the missals of the faithful.

Prayers for Jews should find their inspiration in the common patrimony of Jews and Christians.

Education

Although much study and research remains to be done, in recent years a better understanding of Judaism and its relation to the Church has been gained through the teaching of the Church, scholarly research, and dialogue. In this respect, the following facts should be kept in mind:

(a) It is the One and unique God, who speaks through the Old and New Testaments and gives His promises and gifts "without repentance" (Rom 11:29).

(b) First century Judaism was a complex reality, embodying a world of tendencies, spiritual, religious, social and cultural values, which gave it a character quite different from the Judaism that came after.

(c) The Old Testament and Jewish tradition should not be opposed to the New Testament in such a way as to make it appear as a religion of justice alone, a religion of fear and of legalism, implying that only Christianity possesses the law of love and freedom.

(d) Jesus, as also His disciples, was a Jew. He presented Himself as continuing and fulfilling the anterior Revelation, the basic teachings of which He offered anew, using the same teaching method as the rabbis of His time. The points on which He took issue with the Judaism of His time are fewer than those in which He found Himself in agreement with it. Whenever He opposed it, this was always from within the Jewish people, just as did the prophets before Him.

(e) As to the trial and death of Jesus, Vatican Council II has reminded us that "what happened in Jesus' Passion cannot be blamed upon all the Jews then living, without distinction, nor upon the Jews of today" *(Nostra Aetate).*

(f) The history of Judaism does not end with the destruction of Jerusalem, but continues to develop in a rich spiritual tradition.

(g) According to New Testament teaching, the Jewish people play an essential role in the eschatological fulfillment of history.

The teaching of these data should be extended to all levels of Christian education. Among educational media, the following hold here a particular importance: catechetical manuals, history textbooks, social media of communication (the press, radio, films, television).

The effective use of these means, of course, presupposes a thorough training of teachers and educators in normal schools, seminaries, and universities.

Further research on problems touching upon Judaism and Jewish-Christian relations are to be urged, especially in the fields of exegesis, theology, history, and sociology. Catholic institutions of learning and individual scholars are called upon to contribute toward the elucidation of these problems. Where possible, a chair on Judaism should be established, and collaboration with Jewish scholars encouraged.

Joint Social Action

Jewish and Christian tradition, founded upon the word of God, is deeply conscious of the value of the human person, made in God's image. The love of the same God ought to be translated into efficacious action in the interest of mankind. In the spirit of the prophets, Jews and Christians will collaborate willingly in the pursuit of social justice and peace. This cooperation should extend to local, national, and international levels. And joint action can also work toward a large measure of mutual knowledge and esteem.

Conclusion

Vatican Council II has indicated the path to follow in the rediscovery of a deepened fraternity among Christians and Jews. There remains, nonetheless, a long road ahead.

The problem of Jewish-Christian relations is of concern to the Church as such by the very fact that it is in "searching into its own mystery" that it comes upon the mystery of Israel. The problem hence retains all its importance even in those places where a Jewish community does not exist. Moreover, it includes an ecumenical aspect. Christian churches, in search of the unity willed by the Lord, will find this by a return to the sources and origins of their faith, grafted on the Jewish tradition, which is still living in our own day. In this area, the bishops are invited to take every initiative they consider opportune. They should establish, for example, on national and regional levels, commissions or secretariats, or name a competent person, charged with the responsibility of promoting implementations of the conciliar directives and the suggestions proposed herein.

The Vatican Office for Catholic-Jewish Relations has been established in order to promote and stimulate relations between Christians and Jews. It places itself at the service of all agencies devoted to this work, in order to assist them in their task and to keep them informed, in the hope that by such a collaboration the aims of the Council will be effectively carried out.

In October 1974, Pope Paul set up a Commission for Religious Relations with the Jews.

Guidelines and Suggestions for Implementing the Conciliar Declaration Nostra Aetate *(n. 4), by the Vatican Commission for Religious Relations with the Jews. January 1975.*

The Declaration *Nostra Aetate,* issued by the Second Vatican Council on October 28, 1965, "On the Relationship of the Church to Non-Christian Religions" (n. 4), marks an important milestone in the history of Jewish-Christians relations.

Moreover, the step taken by the Council finds its historical setting in circumstances deeply affected by the memory of the persecution and massacre of Jews which took place in Europe just before and during the Second World War.

Although Christianity sprang from Judaism, taking from it certain essential elements of its faith and divine cult, the gap dividing them was deepened more and more, to such an extent that Christian and Jew hardly knew each other.

After two thousand years, too often marked by mutual ignorance and frequent confrontation, the Declaration *Nostra Aetate* provides an opportunity to open or to continue a dialogue with a view to better mutual understanding. Over the past nine years, many steps in this direction have been taken in various countries. As a result, it is easier to distinguish the conditions under which a new relationship between Jews and Christians may be worked out and developed. This seems the right moment to propose, following the guidelines of the Council, some concrete suggestions born of experience, hoping that they will help to bring into actual existence in the life of the Church the intentions expressed in the conciliar document.

While referring the reader back to this document, we may simply restate here that the spiritual bonds and historical links binding the Church to Judaism condemn (as opposed to the very spirit of Christianity) all forms of anti-Semitism and discrimination, which in any case the dignity of the human person alone would suffice to condemn. Further still, these links and relationships render obligatory a better mutual understanding and renewed mutual esteem. On the practical level in particular, Christians must therefore strive to acquire a better knowledge of the basic components of the religious tradition of Judaism: they must strive to learn by what essential traits the Jews define themselves in the light of their own religious experience.

With due respect for such matters of principle, we simply propose some first practical applications in different essential areas of the Church's life, with a view to launching or developing sound relations between Catholics and their Jewish brothers.

Dialogue

To tell the truth, such relations as there have been between Jew and Christian have scarcely ever risen above the level of monologue. From now on, real dialogue must be established.

Dialogue presupposes that each side wishes to know the other, and wishes to increase and deepen its knowledge of the other. It constitutes a particularly suitable means of favoring a better mutual knowledge and, especially in the case of dialogue between Jews and Christians, of probing the riches of one's own tradition. Dialogue demands respect for the other as he is; above all, respect for his faith and his religious convictions.

In virtue of her divine mission, and her very nature, the Church must preach Jesus Christ to the world *(Ad Gentes,* 2). Lest the witness of Catholics to Jesus Christ should give offence to Jews, they must take care to live and spread their Christian faith while maintaining the strictest respect for religious liberty, in line with the teaching of the Second Vatican Council (Declaration *Dignitatis Humanae).* They will likewise strive to understand the difficulties which arise for the Jewish soul — rightly imbued with an extremely high, pure notion of the divine transcendence — when faced with the mystery of the incarnate Word.

While it is true that a widespread air of suspicion, inspired by an unfortunate past, is still dominant in this particular area, Christians for their part, will be able to see to what extent the responsibility is theirs and deduce practical conclusions for the future.

In addition to friendly talks, competent people will be encouraged to meet and to study together the many problems deriving from the fundamental convictions of Judaism and of Christianity. In order not to hurt (even involuntarily) those taking part, it will be vital to guarantee, not only tact, but a great openness of spirit and diffidence with respect to one's own prejudices.

In whatever circumstances as shall prove possible and mutually acceptable, one might encourage a common meeting in the presence of God, in prayer and silent meditation, a highly efficacious way of finding that humility, that openness of heart and mind, necessary prerequisites for a deep knowledge of oneself and of others. In particular, that will be done in connection with great causes, such as the struggle for peace and justice.

Liturgy

The existing links between the Christian liturgy and the Jewish liturgy will be borne in mind. The idea of a living community in the service of God, and in the service of men for the love of God, such as it is realized in the liturgy, is just as characteristic of the Jewish liturgy as it is of the Christian one. To improve Jewish-Christian relations, it is important to take cognizance of those common elements of the liturgical life (formulas, feasts, rites, etc.) in which the Bible holds an essential place.

An effort will be made to acquire a better understanding of whatever in the Old Testament retains its own perpetual value (cf. *Dei Verbum,* 14-15), since that has not been cancelled by the later interpretation of the New Testament. Rather, the New Testament brings out the full meaning of the Old, while both Old and New illumine and explain each other (cf. *ibid.,* 16). This is all the more important since liturgical reform is now bringing the text of the Old Testament ever more frequently to the attention of Christians.

When commenting on biblical texts, emphasis will be laid on the continuity of our faith with that of the earlier Covenant, in the perspective of the promises, without minimizing those elements of Christianity which are original. We believe that those promises were fulfilled with the first coming of Christ. But it is nonetheless true that we still await their perfect fulfilment in His glorious return at the end of time.

With respect to liturgical readings, care will be taken to see that homilies based on them will not distort their meaning, especially when it is a question of passages which seem to show the Jewish people as such in an unfavorable light. Efforts will be made so to instruct the Christian people that they will understand the true interpretation of all the texts and their meaning for the contemporary believer.

Commissions entrusted with the task of liturgical translation will pay particular attention to the way in which they express those phrases and passages which Christians, if not well informed, might misunderstand because of prejudice. Obviously, one cannot alter the text of the Bible. The point is that, with a version destined for liturgical use, there should be an overriding preoccupation to bring out explicitly the meaning of a text, while taking scriptural studies into account. (Thus the formula "the Jews," in St. John, sometimes according to the context means "the leaders of the Jews," or "the adversaries of Jesus," terms which express better the thought of the Evangelist and avoid appearing to arraign the Jewish people as such. Another example is the use of the words "Pharisee" and "Pharisaism", which have taken on a largely pejorative meaning.)

The preceding remarks also apply to the introductions to biblical readings, to the Prayer of the Faithful, and to commentaries printed in missals used by the laity.

Teaching and Education

Although there is still a great deal of work to be done, a better understanding of Judaism itself and its relationship to Christianity has been achieved in recent years thanks to the teaching of the Church, the study and research of scholars, as also to the beginning of dialogue. In this respect, the following facts deserve to be recalled:

It is the same God, "inspirer and author of the books of both Testaments" *(Dei Verbum, 16)*, who speaks both in the old and new Covenants.

Judaism in the time of Christ and the Apostles was a complex reality, embracing many different trends, many spiritual, religious, social, and cultural values.

The Old Testament and the Jewish tradition founded upon it must not be set against the New Testament in such a way that the former seems to constitute a religion of only justice, fear, and legalism, with no appeal to the love of God and neighbor (cf. Dt 6:5; Lv 19:18; Mt 22:34-40).

Jesus was born of the Jewish people, as were His apostles and a large number of His first disciples. When He revealed Himself as the Messiah and Son (cf. Mt 16:16), the bearer of the new Gospel message, He did so as the fulfilment and perfection of the earlier Revelation. And although His teaching had a profoundly new character, Christ, nevertheless, in many instances, took His stand on the teaching of the Old Testament. The New Testament is profoundly marked by its relation to the Old. As the Second Vatican Council declared: "God, the inspirer and author of the books of both Testaments, wisely arranged that the New Testament be hidden in the Old and the Old be made manifest in the New" *(Dei Verbum, 16)*. Jesus also used teaching methods similar to those employed by the rabbis of His time.

With regard to the trial and death of Jesus, the Council recalled that "what happened in His passion cannot be blamed upon all the Jews then living, without distinction, nor upon the Jews of today" *(Nostra Aetate)*.

The history of Judaism did not end with the destruction of Jerusalem, but rather went on to develop a religious tradition. And, although we believe that the importance and meaning of that tradition were deeply affected by the coming of Christ, it is nonetheless rich in religious values.

With the prophets and the apostle Paul, "the Church awaits the day, known to God alone, on which all peoples will address the Lord in a single voice and serve Him with one accord (Soph 3:9)" *(Nostra Aetate)*.

Information concerning these questions is important at all levels of Christian instruction and education. Among sources of information, special attention should be paid to the following: catechisms and religious textbooks, history books, the mass media (press, radio, movies, television).

The effective use of these means presupposes the thorough formation of instructors and educators in training schools, seminaries, and universities.

Research into the problems bearing on Judaism and Jewish-Christian relations will be encouraged among specialists, particularly in the fields of exegesis, theology, history, and sociology. Higher institutions of Catholic research, in association if possible with other similar Christian institutions and experts, are invited to contribute to the solution of such problems. Wherever possible, chairs of Jewish studies will be created, and collaboration with Jewish scholars encouraged.

Joint Social Action

Jewish and Christian tradition, founded on the word of God, is aware of the value of the human person, the image of God. Love of the same God must show itself in effective action for the good of mankind. In the spirit of the prophets, Jews and Christians will work willingly together, seeking social justice and peace at every level — local, national, and international.

At the same time, such collaboration can do much to foster mutual understanding and esteem.

Conclusion

The Second Vatican Council has pointed out the path to follow in promoting deep fellowship between Jews and Christians. But there is still a long road ahead.

The problem of Jewish-Christian relations concerns the Church as such, since it is when "pondering her own mystery" that she encounters the mystery of Israel. Therefore, even in areas where no Jewish communities exist, this remains an important problem. There is also an ecumenical aspect to the question: the very return of Christians to the sources and origins of their faith, grafted onto the earlier Covenant, helps the search for unity in Christ, the cornerstone.

In this field, the bishops will know what best to do on the pastoral level, within the general disciplinary framework of the Church and in line with the common teaching of her magisterium. For example, they will create some suitable commissions or secretariats on a national or regional level, or appoint some competent person to promote the implementation of the conciliar directives and the suggestions made above.

On October 22, 1974, the Holy Father instituted for the universal Church this Commission for Religious Relations with the Jews, joined to the Secretariat for promoting Christian Unity. This special Commission, created to encourage and foster religious relations between Jews and Catholics — and to do so eventually in collaboration with other Christians — will be, within the limits of its competence, at the service of all interested organizations, providing information for them, and helping them to pursue their task in conformity with the instructions of the Holy See.

b) UNITED STATES STATEMENTS

Guidelines for Catholic-Jewish Relations, U.S. National Conference of Catholic Bishops. March 1967

Perspectives
In its Declaration on the relationship of the Church to Non-Christian Religions of 1965, the Second Vatican Council issued a historic Statement on the Jews and summoned all Catholics to re-appraise their attitude toward, and relationship with the Jewish people.

The Statement was, in effect, a culminating point of initiatives and pronouncements of recent Pontiffs and of numerous endeavors in the Church concerned with Catholic-Jewish harmony. It was also the point of convergence of many insights opened by Pope Paul's Encyclical *Ecclesiam Suam* and the Council's Constitution on the Church and Decree on Ecumenism.

The call of the Council to a fraternal encounter with Jews may be seen, further, as one of the more important fruits of the spirit of renewal generated by the Council in its deliberations and decrees. Was it not indeed the Council's response to Pope John XXIII's famous words in which he embraced the Jewish people: "I am Joseph your brother"? (Gen 45:4).
More specifically, the Council's call is an acknowledgement of the conflicts and tensions that have separated Christians and Jews through the centuries and of the Church's determination, as far as possible, to eliminate

them. Well does it serve both in word and action as a recognition of the manifold sufferings and injustices inflicted upon the Jewish people by Christians in our own times as well as in the past. The Statement speaks from the highest level of the Church's authority to serve notice that injustices directed against the Jews at any time from any source can never receive Catholic sanction or support.

The message of the Council's statement is clear. Recalling in moving terms the "spiritual bond that ties the people of the New Covenant to Abraham's stock," the Fathers of the Council remind us of the special place Jews hold in the Christian outlook, for "now as before God holds them as most dear for the sake of the patriarchs; He has not withdrawn His gifts or calling." Jews, therefore, the Fathers caution, are not "to be presented as rejected or accursed by God, as if this followed from holy scripture." The Passion of Jesus, moreover, "cannot be attributed without distinction to all Jews then alive, nor can it be attributed to the Jews of today." The Church, the Statement declares, "decries hatred, persecutions, displays of anti-Semitism directed against the Jews at any time and by anyone." In light of these principles the Fathers enjoin that "all see to it that nothing is taught, either in catechetic work or in the preaching of the Word of God that does not conform to the truth of the Gospel and the spirit of Christ."

Rather should Christians and Jews "further their mutual knowledge of and respect for one another, a knowledge and respect deriving primarily from biblical and theological studies and fraternal dialogues."

Responding to the urgency of the Conciliar Statement on the Jews, our American Bishops have established, as part of their Committee for Ecumenical and Interreligious Affairs, a Sub-committee for Catholic-Jewish Relations. This Sub-committee will devote itself exclusively to Catholic-Jewish affairs. The guidelines which follow, composed by the Sub-commission, are designed to encourage and assist the various dioceses of the country in their efforts to put into action at all levels of the Church the Council's directives.

The Church in America is faced with a historic opportunity to advance the cause of Catholic-Jewish harmony throughout the world — an opportunity to continue the leadership taken in that direction by our American Bishops during the great debate on the Statement at the Council. In the United States lives the largest Jewish community in the world. In the United States, a land that has welcomed immigrants and refugees from persecution, the Church has committed herself without reserve to the American ideal of equal opportunity and justice for all. In such a setting the Church in America today is providentially situated to distinguish itself in pursuit of the purposes of the Council's Statement.

It is our prayerful hope that the norms and recommendations of these guidelines will prove helpful to American Catholics in attaining this noble objective.

General Principles

1. It is recommended that in each diocese in which Jews and Christians live a commission or secretariat, or some member thereof, be assigned to Catholic-Jewish affairs.

2. In keeping with the spirit of the Council's Declaration on Ecumenism, Catholics should take the initiative not only in Catholic-Protestant and Orthodox affairs, but also in fostering Catholic-Jewish understanding. Public and formal projects, however, should have the approval of the Ordinary of the diocese.

3. The general aim of all Catholic-Jewish meetings is to increase our understanding both of Judaism and the Catholic faith, eliminate sources of tension and misunderstanding, initiate dialogues or conversations on different levels, multiply intergroup meetings between Catholics and Jews, and promote cooperative social action.

4. These meetings should be marked by a genuine respect for the person and freedom of all participants and a willingness to listen and to learn from the other party. They should be jointly planned and developed.

5. In order to avoid possible apprehensions concerning the objectives of these meetings, their scope and confines should be mutually agreed upon in advance.

6. It is recommended that in order to maintain the dialogue on the highest possible level its organization be accomplished in consultation with those experienced in the structural, doctrinal, and inter-personal skills which the dialogue requires.

7. It is understood that proselytizing is to be carefully avoided in the dialogue, the chief aim of which, as Cardinal Bea has pointed out in his *The Church and the Jewish People,* "is not specifically concerned with the differences between Christianity and other religions. That is to say, with the characteristic features of the former, but rather with the points which it has in common with other faiths."

8. Prayer in common with Jews should, whenever it is feasible, be encouraged, especially in matters of common concern, such as peace and the welfare of the community. Needless to say, such prayers should meet the spiritual sensibilities of both parties, finding their inspiration in our common faith in the One God.

Recommended Programs

1. Catholic-Jewish relations should be advanced on all levels; clerical and

lay, academic and popular, religious and social.

2. A favored instrument is the dialogue, a form of group conversation in which competent participants discuss assigned topics or themes in openness, candor, and friendship. Those not well versed in inter-religious affairs run the risk of unwittingly offending by inaccurate portrayal of each other's doctrine or way of life.

3. Diocesan and parochial organizations, schools, colleges, universities, and especially seminaries should organize programs to implement the Statement.

4. The pulpit should also be used for expounding the teachings of the Statement and exhorting participation in programs fitted to the parochial level.

5. School texts, prayerbooks, and other media should, under competent auspices be examined in order to remove not only those materials which do not accord with the content and spirit of the Statement, but also those which fail to show Judaism's role in salvation-history in any positive light.

6. It is recommended that Catholic-Jewish understanding be fostered effectively at the popular level by means of so-called "open houses" in places of worship, mutual visits to schools, joint social events, and "living room dialogues."

7. Catholic-Jewish cooperation in the field of social action designed to promote public welfare and morality should be encouraged.

8. Orientation and resource material for the foregoing recommendations may be sought from the various Catholic and Jewish organizations that have been active in the field of Christian-Jewish relations. It is also suggested that contact be made with Protestant agencies and leadership experts in this area of endeavor.

9. While popular "grassroots" programs to improve Catholic-Jewish relations must be pressed foward without delay, slower and deeper explorations of pertinent issues by Catholic and Jewish scholars must also be given a high priority. Since many of the problems in this area of Catholic-Jewish relations are intellectual in nature, research in history, psychology, sociology, and the Bible by individual Catholic and Jewish scholars as well as collaborative scholarly enterprises are to be highly commended.

10. The following themes which, among others, are viewed by Christian and Jewish experts as important issues affecting Christian-Jewish relations merit the attention and study of Catholic educators and scholars:

a. Scholarly studies and educational efforts to show the common historical, biblical, doctrinal and liturgical heritage shared by Catholics and Jews, as well as their differences.

b. As the Statement requires, the presentation of the Crucifixion story in such a way as not to implicate all Jews of Jesus' time or of today in a collective guilt for the crime.

c. In keeping with the Statement's strong repudiation of anti-Semitism, a frank and honest treatment of the history of Christian anti-Semitism in our history books, courses, and curricula.

d. A study of the life of Jesus and of the primitive Church in the setting of the religious, social, and cultural features of Jewish life in the first century.

e. An explicit rejection of the historically inaccurate notion that Judaism of that time, especially Pharisaism, was a decadent formalism and hypocrisy, well exemplified by Jesus' enemies.

f. An acknowledgment by Catholic scholars of the living and complex reality of Judaism after Christ and the permanent election of Israel, alluded to by St. Paul (Rom 9:29), and incorporation of the results into Catholic teaching.

g. A full and precise explanation of the use of the expression "the Jews" by St. John and other New Testament references which appear to place all Jews in a negative light. (These expressions and references should be fully and precisely clarified in accordance with the intent of the Statement that Jews are not to be "presented as rejected or accursed by God as if this followed from holy scripture.")

Guidelines for the Advancement of Catholic-Jewish Relations in the Archdiocese of New York, Diocese of Rockville Centre, Diocese of Brooklyn. 1969.

Preface

When Pope John XXIII welcomed a group of Jews who had come to demonstrate their affection for him, he spoke that now famous salutation "I am Joseph your brother" (Gn 45:4). With these words he embraced the whole Jewish people. Behind that spontaneous greeting was a vision that has continued to grow in the Church's teaching and practice during the reign of Pope Paul VI.

The teaching of Vatican II speaks in the categories of brotherly love suggested by Pope John when it recalls "the spiritual bond linking the people of the New Covenant with Abraham's stock" *(Nostra Aetate, n. 4)*. It sees clearly that the roots of the relationship between Christianity and Judaism are to be found in the common fatherhood of Abraham. It calls upon the Church to recognize the workings of God's mysterious providence by reminding her that she must see her own beginnings in the faith and election of the patriarchs, Moses and the prophets.

The Church ever keeps in mind the words of the Apostle about his kinsmen "who have the adoption as sons, and the glory and the covenant and the legislation and the worship and the promises" (Rom. 9:4). Indeed, many of the specific elements of her faith from which the Church derives her very life are foreshadowed in Israel's history: baptism in the passage through the sea; the Eucharist in the manna; Christ Himself in the cloud, the pillar of fire and the rock that yielded lifegiving water at Moses' insistent command (cf. I Cor 10:1-5).

For all of these reasons the Church loves the Jewish people and recognizes that they "remain most dear to God, for God does not repent of the gifts He makes nor of the calls He issues" *(Lumen Gentium,* 16). With Pope Pius XI we proudly reaffirm that "spiritually we are all Semites."

Aware of this rich heritage, and the close ties with the Jewish Community that it implies, we the Bishops of the Archdiocese of New York and the Dioceses of Brooklyn and Rockville Centre offer these Guidelines for Catholic-Jewish Relations. We do so in the hope that they may foster a deeper spirit of fraternal understanding and love, and that they may prove a valuable instrument of mutual cooperation leading to a reassertion in our time of the religious and social values of the Judaeo-Christian tradition.

We are conscious of the fact that in our three Dioceses we have one of the largest Jewish Communities in the world — almost two and a half million persons. This circumstance imposes on us the special responsibility as well as offers us the opportunity to engage in a program of exchange of knowledge, respect and affection with our Jewish brothers.

It is our hope that the principles and practical suggestions of these Guidelines find a ready acceptance in every heart and an effective implementation in every parish, school and organ of our three Dioceses.

We are gratified that the preparation of these Guidelines is the collective effort of members of our three Ecumenical Commissions because we feel that a uniform approach to the work of Catholic-Jewish Relations will produce more effective results. And finally, we wish to acknowledge in a special way the assistance of members of the Jewish Community who have given us the benefit of their scholarly and critical evaluation.

General Principles
1. The general aim of all Catholic-Jewish programs is to increase mutual understanding between Jews and Catholics, to eliminate sources of misunderstanding and tension, and to promote that cooperation which reflects our common religious bonds by the initiation and development of inter-religious meetings at all levels.

2. The formation of permanent diocesan committees composed of priests, religious, laymen and women, together with rabbis and Jewish laymen and women, should be greatly encouraged. These units could then proceed to implement recommended activities.

3. All programs should be marked by a genuine respect for the person and freedom of all particulars and a willingness to learn from the other party.

All such programs should be jointly planned and developed.

4.   There should be a prior consensus on the objectives, scope and confines of these programs, and all encounters should be worked out in a spirit of mutuality.

5.   A favored instrument in promoting Catholic-Jewish understanding is the dialogue, a form of group conversation in which the participants discuss assigned topics or themes. In order to initiate and maintain a dialogue between the two Communities most effectively, experts in theology, social organization and interpersonal skills should be consulted.

6.   Conscious of the challenge of modern society to religion, we view this dialogue and all other common efforts as effective means to reaffirm the religious traditions of Judaism and Christianity, and to strengthen the commitment of both Communities to their own religious heritage.

7.   We reaffirm here the statement made by the National Conference of Catholic Bishops in their Guidelines for Catholic-Jewish Relations: that "proselytizing is to be carefully avoided in the dialogue."

8.   Catholic-Jewish Relations should be advanced on all levels, clerical and lay, academic and popular, religious and social. Participation in these activities should be of such a nature that it will strengthen the commitment of the participants to their own religious traditions.

9.   We place high value on fraternal encounters between priests and rabbis as individual religious leaders, as well as on the development of a friendly rapport with the various rabbinical associations.

10.   Equal stress should be placed on a cooperative association with organizations within the Jewish Community which play an important role in furthering Jewish ideals of service, charity and inter-religious harmony through laudable programs in all areas of education and social action.

Recommended Activities

1.   A favored activity is the dialogue described previously in "General Principles." It should be conducted in a spirit of openness, candor and friendship. Our efforts should aim at an extended dialogue in order to achieve a deeper understanding of the living faith of the participants.

2.   The following forms of dialogue are recommended:

   a.   Institutes for priests and rabbis, which afford religious leaders the opportunity to hear scholars of both Communities discuss their common heritage and basic differences, with the added advantage of group discussions.

   b.   Institutes for lay leaders of both Communities, with themes suitable to their competence and interests.

   c.   Community dialogues at the popular or "grassroots" level among well-prepared participants with the cooperation of the religious leaders of both Communities.

d. Special educational programs held generally under the sponsorship of Catholic high schools, colleges and universities in collaboration with Jewish organizations.

3. The religious leaders of both Communities are reminded that their pulpit offers a powerful means of advancing mutual understanding, friendship and cooperation.

4. Catholic-Jewish understanding can also be effectively fostered at the popular level by so-called "open houses" in the places of worship, mutual visits to educational institutions and joint social events.

5. Competent priests, religious, laymen and women are encouraged to accept invitations from Jewish congregations and organizations to explain Catholic doctrine, liturgical worship, sacramental practice, moral problems and social doctrine. All semblance of debate should be avoided.

Catholic religious leaders are also encouraged to extend invitations to rabbis and Jewish lay leaders to participate in explanations of Jewish beliefs and practices.

If a Catholic is invited to take part in a radio or television program, or in a public discussion, it is recommended that he consult the appropriate diocesan ecumenical commission.

6. Jewish and Catholic clergy may address gatherings in which Catholics and Jews join in prayer for some common objective such as peace, social justice, brotherhood, or to ask God's blessing on the occasion of national holidays and other times when the public invocation of God is fitting. Permission is granted to preach before or after a liturgical service, but not during any specifically liturgical service.

7. Prayer in common with Jews should be encouraged wherever it is mutually acceptable, specifically in matters of common concern, such as peace and the welfare of the community. Such prayers should take account of the spiritual sensibilities of both Communities and find inspiration in their common faith in the One God.

8. It is recommended that public prayers for the welfare of the Jewish Community be included in our liturgical celebrations. In particular, it is appropriate that the intentions of individual members of the Jewish Community be included, on occasion, in the Prayer of the Faithful.

9. On occasion Catholics may accept invitations to attend the liturgical services of Jewish congregations (e.g. the Sabbath services, weddings, Bar Mitzvahs) for reasons such as public office, blood or marriage relationship, friendship, etc. In choosing the proper attire, priests should consider the practice of the congregation and, where necessary, consult the rabbi.

10. In a spirit of reciprocity, Jewish religious and lay leaders who might

wish to attend a Catholic liturgical celebration should be made welcome. On appropriate occasions they should be given a place of honor in the sanctuary.

11. Jewish religious and lay leaders should be invited to important diocesan and parochial events. Conversely, Catholic clergy and laity are encouraged to accept invitations of the same nature extended by the Jewish Community.

12. Catholic-Jewish cooperation should be encouraged in the field of social action in order to promote public welfare. Such cooperation should contribute to a just appreciation of the human person, the promotion of peace, and the application of Judaeo-Christian principles to social life and its institutions. It should be pursued in a spirit of sensitivity to the deepest spiritual, moral and cultural values.

13. This cooperation should include the coordination of efforts to promote world peace, racial justice and civil rights, to combat poverty, to extend and improve educational facilities, to reduce the cause of delinquency, to relieve the victims of disaster and to help resolve other civic problems.

14. Catholic diocesan and parish organizations as well as individuals should be encouraged to collaborate with Jewish organizations and individuals which provide services in the fields of health, education and welfare.

15. Diocesan and parochial organizations, religious communities, educational institutions, especially seminaries, should organize programs to implement the teaching of Vatican II on the Jews, to the U.S. Bishops' Guidelines and local Guidelines.

16. School texts, prayerbooks and other media should be subject to constant scrutiny in order to avoid any materials which do not accord with the content and spirit of the Vatican Council's teachings. At the same time, an earnest effort should be made to insert those teachings which show Judaism's role in salvation-history in a positive light.

Areas of Special Interest
1. It is understood that in the difficult situation of a marriage between a Catholic and a Jew, courtesy and charity will characterize the attitude of all priests.

2. Should a rabbi accept the invitation extended to him by a Catholic couple being married in a Catholic Church, he should be offered a place of honor in the sanctuary. At the request of the bridal couple, he might be invited to speak some words of congratulation and exhortation to the couple, after the Catholic ceremony. He may also be asked to invoke God's blessing on the couple.

3. In the same spirit, a Catholic priest is permitted to attend the marriage of two Jewish people by a rabbi, provided that the marriage would be regarded as valid in Catholic law. At the request of the bridal couple, and with the permission of the rabbi, he might accept an invitation to speak some words of congratulation and exhortation to the couple, after the Jewish ceremony. Again, with the permission of the rabbi, he might invoke God's blessing on the couple.

4. Jews may be admitted as witnesses and attendants at a marriage ceremony in a Catholic Church provided they meet the standard requirements.

5. When invited, Catholics may serve as witnesses at civil weddings of friends who belong to the Jewish community, provided that the weddings to be witnessed will be lawful and valid according to Catholic law, and provided that they take place within the dioceses in which these regulations are in effect.

6. Most Jewish funerals are held in funeral homes, which are not houses of worship, even though they are sometimes called "chapels." A funeral service is held in the Synagogue on very rare occasions, for an outstanding Jewish scholar, rabbi, or community leader. In either case, it is advisable that priests come in their clerical street attire, and not in their liturgical vesture.

7. According to immemorial Jewish custom, a period of mourning called *Shiva* is held at the home of the deceased or of his closest kin. It is certainly very proper for Catholic friends of the deceased or of the family to visit during this week of mourning in order to give comfort and sympathy to the bereaved. Contributions to a favorite charity of the family of the deceased are considered to be an expression of neighborly concern, of friendship and of sympathy for the bereaved.

8. Catholic hosts should be prepared to take into consideration the religious dietary laws which may be observed by Jewish guests, at any function to which Jewish individuals or groups are invited, and at which refreshments are part of the program.

Themes for Catholics Engaged in the Dialogue
Because of its importance and practical value, we reprint in full Section 1-Paragraphs A to G of "Recommended Programs" contained in the text of the U.S. Bishops' *Guidelines for Catholic-Jewish Relations*. The selection of themes listed below and the extent to which they are pursued are left to the discretion of each diocesan commission.

The following themes which, among others, are viewed by Christians and Jews engaged in the dialogue as important issues affecting Christian-Jewish relations merit the attention and study of Catholic educators and scholars.

a. Scholarly studies and educational efforts to show the common, historical, biblical, doctrinal and liturgical heritage shared by Catholics and Jews, as well as their differences.

b. As the statement requires, the presentation of the Crucifixion story in such a way as not to implicate all Jews of Jesus' time or of today in a collective guilt for the crime.

c. In keeping with the statement's strong repudiation of anti-Semitism, a frank and honest treatment of the history of Christian anti-Semitism in our history books, courses and curricula.

d A study of the life of Jesus and of the primitive church in the setting of the religious, social, and cultural features of Jewish life in the first century.

e. An explicit rejection of the historically inaccurate notion that Judaism of that time, especially that of Pharisaism, was a decadent formalism and hypocrisy, well exemplified by Jesus' enemies.

f. An acknowledgement by Catholic scholars of the living and complex reality of Judaism after Christ and the permanent election of Israel, alluded by St. Paul (Rom 9:29), and incorporation of the results into Catholic teaching.

g. A full and precise explanation of the use of the expression "the Jews" by St. John and other New Testament references which appear to place all Jews in a negative light. (These expressions and references should be fully and precisely clarified in accordance with the intent of the Statement that Jews are not to be "presented as rejected or accursed by God as if this followed from Holy Scripture.")

The Formation of Diocesan Committees

The following suggestions may be of value in the formation and operation of Catholic-Jewish Relations committees with diocesan sponsorship:

1. The establishment of an official, permanent committee will give consistency and continuity to the work of Catholic-Jewish relations, and avoid haphazard, unrelated efforts.

2. The committee should be composed of priests, religious, laymen and women, together with rabbis. Jewish laymen and women, who have some organizational experience and at least a basic knowledge of the Jewish and Catholic Communities. The size of the committee will depend on the size of the Jewish community in the diocese and on local needs.

3. Catholic members of the committee may be appointed to membership on the diocesan ecumenical commission if they are assigned to the special sub-committee for Catholic-Jewish relations.

4. Appointment of committee members by the Ordinary will lend prestige and authority to the committee and increase its effectiveness.

5. Since the work of the committee is a mutual effort, a priest and a rabbi should be co-chairmen, and the post of executive secretary should be shared by a member from each faith.

6. The committee will be more effective if the rabbinical members are representatives of the Orthodox, Conservative and Reform areas of Judaism, and if the Jewish laymen are members of some of the principal Jewish lay organizations.

7. Once established, the diocesan committee should plan a schedule of regular meetings each year. These meetings could have this two-fold purpose: a) the education of the members themselves by frequent presentations and discussions of topics of basic interest, and b) the preparation of a series of programs in the spirit of those suggested by these Guidelines.

The Formation of Local Councils

After the diocesan Catholic-Jewish Relations committee has been established and is functioning efficiently, serious consideration could be given to the formation of local *Catholic-Jewish Councils* which bring this work to the community level.

While at present this type of endeavor is relatively new and our experience rather limited, the following steps are suggested for the formation of local *Councils:*

1. The diocesan committee should stimulate the idea of local *Councils* in various areas of the diocese.

2. The Committee should encourage the establishment of *Councils,* starting with areas most receptive to the idea, and where there is the greatest chance of success.

3. The diocesan committee should offer its assistance and cooperation to local groups which volunteer to start a *Council.*

4. When *Councils* are established, the diocesan committee should keep a friendly liaison with them and seek to coordinate their activities.

5. If the structure of the local *Council* follows the pattern of the parent diocesan committee, it would help if the two co-chairmen of the *Council* were invited to serve as representatives to the diocesan committee.

It is likely that, with the growth in the number of these *Councils* and the resulting gain in experience, more information may be supplied later in the form of an addendum to these Guidelines.

*Guidelines for Catholic-Jewish Relations in the
Diocese of Albany, New York. 1970.*

*(These Guidelines are modeled on those of the New
York Archdiocese and are excerpted.)*

......It is recommended that each parish expand its existing Ecumenical Committee to include inter-religious affairs. The local committees would thereby follow the pattern of the Diocesan Commission. We recommend that the committees proceed to implement these guide-lines and keep a friendly liaison with the Diocesan Jewish Communities Committee. We recommend that the parish committee be represented on the parish council. ......Priests witnessing a marriage between a Catholic and a Jew are asked to use the new rite of marriage for a "Catholic and a non-baptized person." ......The Jewish Communities Committee is the official diocesan organ for the furtherance of Catholic-Jewish relations. It is one of the standing committees of the Diocesan Commission for Ecumenical and Interreligious Affairs.

*Document on Ecumenism. Relations with other Religions
and with Non-Believers. Archdiocese of Cincinnati, Ohio. 1971.*

*(These Guidelines are modeled on those of the New York
Archdiocese and are excerpted.)*

......Because of the presence of an active Jewish community and a leading Hebrew seminary in Cincinnati, our relations with Judaism are of primary importance and offer us an exceptional opportunity "to advance the cause of Catholic-Jewish harmony......"
......We must remember that before a real bond of understanding can exist between Roman Catholics and Jews, the task of examining our shared history is mandatory. The Nazi holocaust and the establishment of the State of Israel force us to look with compassion and candor on the magnitude of these two events. We are also challenged to examine two thousand years of vilification and persecution which have laid the burden of proving good faith on the Christian's shoulders. For the future, a continued concern for the integrity of the individual conscience as well as a respect for the person should cause all Roman Catholics to abhor any manifestation of anti-Semitism, even as it may appear in our society today.

When approaching the Jewish community in order to initiate and implement these guidelines, Roman Catholics must remember that there is a divergence of views among Jews as there is among Christians. Judaism, too, is experiencing the initial efforts towards an ecumenism of the three major Jewish communities of faith. Actually, the distinction between these three communities is more in degree than in principle. They all authenticate themselves in God and the Jewish tradition. The authenticity of Orthodox

Judaism is premised on continued adherence to the full range of Jewish observances as they have been created, with preservation being the keynote. Conversative Judaism acknowledges much the same principles as those of Orthodoxy but also recognizes a certain developmental character of tradition and, with great caution and respect, will pass judgment on certain traditional rulings of the past. Reform Judaism recognizes the preservative, the developmental, and the innovative as all part of the Jewish tradition and can use traditions as process and as tool. Because of this diversity of views in Judaism itself, Roman Catholics must expect from Jewish congregations a varied range of participation.

.......Roman Catholics will gain a deeper appreciation of Christ's life and the sacraments He instituted by experiencing and understanding Jewish holidays. The possibility of joint celebration of these holidays should be explored.

"Open houses" between congregations may be a means of promoting good will and understanding between Jews and Roman Catholics.

.......A correct relation to the Jewish people can never come about as long as Roman Catholics feel strangers to the Bible .... The history of persecution should not be concealed and the Jewish people should not be treated as though they were non-existent.

.......Since Jewish worship is an affirmation of monotheism and a community affirmation, it is considered desirable to bring Jews and Christians together for prayers. Whenever possible and mutually desirable, meeting before God in prayer and silent meditation should be encouraged ......It is indicated in particular when dealing with major questions of reparation, reconciliation, and in times of persecution.

.......Today a new severance between the sacred and the secular has emerged in parts of our society. In this climate, Christians would do well to remember the Jewish concept of a sort of "consecration" of the universe. Judaism recognizes that man is not only creature but avows that man is also co-creator when he acts with God in a continuing creation of the universe.

Remembering that Christ's miracles can be viewed as a kind of social healing and that social involvement is part and parcel of the Jew's ministrations to all his fellow men, Roman Catholics should seek to cooperate with Jews individually and through organizations in order to work toward the solutions of social problems.

.......Roman Catholics should strive to understand the concern of the Jewish community for the State of Israel and should seek to support efforts that will ensure a just and lasting peace in the Holy Land for all concerned.

Statement on Catholic-Jewish Relations by the U.S. National Conference of Catholic Bishops, November, 1975.

Ten years have passed since the Second Vatican Council promulgated its statement on the Jewish people (*Nostra Aetate,* no. 4). This decade has been a period unique in Catholic-Jewish relations. The vantage point of ten years later provides a timely opportunity for the Catholic Church in the United States to recall, reaffirm and reflect on the principles and teachings of the conciliar document, and to evaluate their implementation in our country.

For this task we welcome the new Guidelines and Suggestions for implementing *Nostra Aetate*, no. 4 issued in January of this year by the Commission for Religious Relations with the Jews recently established by the Holy See. And we are reminded of the still very applicable programs recommended by the Guidelines for Catholic-Jewish Relations which our National Conference of Catholic Bishops issued in 1967. We are gratified that the latter have been highly regarded, especially in the Jewish community, and that some of their recommendations anticipated portions of the new Guidelines of the Holy See and also of several diocesan documents.

These two documents, themselves fruits of *Nostra Aetate*, no. 4, elucidate the conciliar declaration, considerably extend its perspectives and broaden the paths it opened. Both are eloquent testimonies to the new horizons the Second Vatican Council succeeded in bringing into Catholic view.

These ten years make it clear that *Nostra Aetate*, no. 4 initiated a new era in Catholic-Jewish affairs. Calling for "fraternal dialogue and biblical studies" with Jews, it ended a centuries-long silence between Church and Synagogue. An age of dialogue was begun. Conversations between Catholics and Jews proliferated rapidly in many forms. Productive meetings took place on every level, from the highest intellectual exchanges to the most popular types of social gatherings, often referred to as "living room dialogues." Our own Bishops' Conference was among the first to form a national commission which sought to implement the Council document. Even before the close of the Second Vatican Council in 1965, the United States Bishops had decided to establish a commission in the National Conference of Catholic Bishops to promote Catholic-Jewish understanding, and in 1967 the first full-time Secretariat for Catholic-Jewish relations was in operation.

Since that time the Secretariat has maintained fruitful contact with the major groups within the Jewish community and has been in regular communication with the dioceses of the country. Many dioceses have followed the example of our Conference and have established Commissions or Secretariats for Jewish-Catholic relations. Numerous projects have been undertaken, including, for example, a careful and systematic analysis of Catholic teaching texts in order to eliminate offensive references to Jews and replace them with materials showing Judaism in a positive light. Numerous theological discussions have been undertaken and Catholic collaboration with the Jewish community has resulted in a variety of social action programs. We are pleased to observe that many of these initiatives have been emulated on the unofficial level by many individuals and groups across the country who have shown admirable sensitivity, dedication and expertise in promoting Catholic-Jewish amity.

We do not wish to convey the impression that all our problems are behind us. There still exist areas of disagreement and misunderstanding which create tensions in both communities. We hope that the difficulties can be resolved to some degree in amicable discussion. Certainly the Catholic view on aid to non-public schools should be the subject of serious dialogue and concern. We are pleased that this and other exchanges have already been held on important subjects of disagreement, and it is our hope that progress will be made in mutual understanding by furthering this dialogic method.

Recalling past centuries, however, invites a sobering evaluation of our progress and warns against becoming over-confident about an early end to remaining problems. Those were centuries replete with alienation, misunderstanding and hostility between Jews and Christians. While we rejoice that there are signs that anti-Semitism is declining in our country, conscience compels us to confront with candor the unhappy record of Jewish suffering both past and present. We make our own the statement of *Nostra Aetate*, ".......for the sake of her common patrimony with the Jews, the Church decries hatred, persecutions, displays of anti-Semitism staged against Jews at whatever time in history and by whomsoever" and we reaffirm with the new Vatican Guidelines that "the spiritual bonds and historical links binding the Church to Judaism condemn (as opposed to the very spirit of Christianity) all forms of anti-Semitism......." We urge all in the Church who work in the area of education, whether in the seminary, the school or the pulpit, not only to avoid any presentation that might tend to disparage Jews or Judaism but also to emphasize those aspects of our faith which bear witness to our common patrimony and our spiritual ties with Jews.

Much of the alienation between Christian and Jew found its origins in a certain anti-Judaic theology which over the centuries has led not only to social friction with Jews but often to their oppression. One of the most hopeful developments in our time, powerfully assisted by *Nostra Aetate*, has been the decline of the old anti-Judaism and the reformation of Christian theological expositions of Judaism along more constructive lines.

The first major step in this direction was the repudiation of the charge that Jews were and are collectively guilty of the death of Christ. *Nostra Aetate* and the new Guidelines have definitely laid to rest this myth which has caused so much suffering to the Jewish people. There remains however the continuing task of ensuring that nothing which in any way approaches the notion of Jewish collective guilt should be found in any Catholic medium of expression or communication. Correctly viewed, the disappearance of the charge of collective guilt of Jews pertains as much to the purity of the Catholic faith as it does to the defense of Judaism.

The Council's rejection of this charge against Jews has been interpreted by some commentators as an "exoneration" of the Jewish people. Such a view of the matter still persists. The truth is that the Council acknowledged that the Jewish people never were, nor are they now, guilty of the death of Christ.

Nostra Aetate was a new beginning in Catholic-Jewish relations and, as with all beginnings, we are faced with the task of revising some traditional understandings and judgments. The brief suggestions of the Council document have been taken up by some theologians, but their implications for theological renewal have not yet been fully explored. We therefore make a few recommendations in line with two themes of the document: the Jewish origins of the Church and the thought of St. Paul.

Christians have not fully appreciated their Jewish roots. Early in Christian history a de-Judaizing process dulled our awareness of our Jewish beginnings. The Jewishness of Jesus, of his mother, his disciples, of the primitive Church, was lost from view. That Jesus was called Rabbi; that he was born, lived and died under the Law; that He and Peter and Paul worshipped in the Temple - these facts were blurred by the controversy that alienated Christians from the Synagogue. How Jewish the Church was toward midpoint of the first century is dramatically reflected in the description of the "Council of Jerusalem" (Acts 15). The question at issue was whether Gentile converts to the Church had to be circumcised and observe the Mosaic Law? The obligation to obey the Law was held so firmly by the Jewish Christians of that time that miraculous visions accorded to Peter and Cornelius (Acts 10) were needed to vindicate the contrary contention that Gentile Christians were not so obliged. By the third century, however, a de-Judaizing process had set in which tended to undervalue the Jewish origins of the Church, a tendency that has surfaced from time to time in devious ways throughout Christian history. Some catechists, homilists, and teachers still convey little appreciation of the Jewishness of that heritage and rich spirituality which we derive from Abraham, Moses, the prophets, the psalmists, and other spiritual giants of the Hebrew Scriptures.

Most essential concepts in the Christian creed grew at first in Judaic soil. Uprooted from that soil, these basic concepts cannot be perfectly understood. It is for reasons such as these that *Nostra Aetate* recommends joint "theological and biblical studies" with Jews. The Vatican Guidelines of 1975 encourage Catholic specialists to engage in new research into the relations of Judaism and Christianity and to seek out "collaboration with Jewish scholars." The renewal of Christian faith is the issue here, for renewal always entails to some extent a return to one's origins.

The Council document cites St. Paul, particularly in chapters 9 to 11 of his Letter to the Romans. We find in these rediscovered, precious chapters Paul's love for his kinsmen and a firm basis for Christian reverence for the Jewish people. Admittedly, Paul's theology of Judaism has its more negative aspects; they have been adequately emphasized over the centuries in

Catholic teaching. It would be well today to explore and emphasize the positive elements of Paul's thought that have received inadequate attention.

In these chapters Paul reveals his deep love of the Jewish people. He tells of his willingness to accept damnation itself for the sake of his kinsmen (9:3), even though he also expresses his painful disappointment and incomprehension at Israel's failure to accept Jesus as its Messiah. Crucial to an understanding of his admiration of the Jewish people and to a Christian understanding of their situation is the following text. Written at the midpoint of the first century, Paul refers to his "kinsmen according to the flesh who are Israelites, who have the adoption as sons, and the glory and the covenants and the legislation and the worship and the promises; who have the fathers, and from whom is the Christ according to the flesh" (9:3-5), thus making clear the continuing validity of Israel's call. Paul, moreover, insists that God has by no means rejected his people. "Is it possible that God has rejected his people? Of course not. I, an Israelite descended from Abraham through the tribe of Benjamin, could never agree that God has rejected his people, the people he chose specially long ago" (11:1-2). What proof does Paul offer for the enduring validity of Israel's relationship to God even after the founding of the Church? "God never takes back his gifts or revokes his choice" (11:29).

Paul warns fellow Christians against showing contempt for the Jewish people by reminding them that they (Christians) are wild branches grafted into the olive tree itself to share its life. "....remember that you do not support the root: it is the root that supports you" (11:18). And he invites his listeners to a love of the Jews, since they are "still loved by God for the sake of their ancestors" (11:28).

In effect, we find in the Epistle to the Romans (9-11) long-neglected passages which help us to construct a new and positive attitude toward the Jewish people. There is here a task incumbent on theologians, as yet hardly begun, to explore the continuing relationship of the Jewish people with God and their spiritual bonds with the New Covenant and the fulfillment of God's plan for both Church and Synagogue.

To revere only the ancient Jewish patriarchs and prophets is not enough. The all too common view of Judaism as a legalistic and decadent form of religion that lost all significance with the coming of Christ and all vitality after the destruction of the Temple has lingered on in the Christian centuries. The 1975 Guidelines put us on guard against such a view and urge us to see post-biblical Judaism as rich in religious values and worthy of our sincere respect and esteem. The Guidelines in fact discourage us from attempting to define the Jews in exclusively Christian terms, explicitly stating, "dialogue demands respect for the other as he is" (Part 1). Again, "Christians must therefore strive to acquire a better knowledge of the basic components of the religious tradition of Judaism: they must strive to learn by what essential traits the Jews define themselves in the light of their own religious experience" (Introduction).

In dialogue with Christians, Jews have explained that they do not consider themselves as a church, a sect, or a denomination, as is the case among Christian communities, but rather as a peoplehood that is not solely racial, ethnic or religious, but in a sense a composite of all these. It is for such reasons that an overwhelming majority of Jews see themselves bound in one way or another to the land of Israel. Most Jews see this tie to the land as essential to their Jewishness. Whatever difficulties Christians may experience in sharing this view they should strive to understand this link between land and people which Jews have expressed in their writings and worship throughout two millenia as a longing for the homeland, holy Zion. Appreciation of this link is not to give assent to any particular religious interpretation of this bond. Nor is this affirmation meant to deny the legitimate rights of other parties in the region, or to adopt any political stance in the controversies over the Middle East, which lie beyond the purview of this statement.

On this tenth anniversary of *Nostra Aetate* we reaffirm our wholehearted commitment to the principles of that document as well as to the directives of the Guidelines of 1975. Aware of the magnitude of the task before us and of the excellence of the many practical guidelines and suggestions contained in the documents, we urge that special attention be given to the following exhortations:

1.   That all dioceses, according to their needs and circumstances, create and support whatever instrument or agency is appropriate for carrying out the recommendations of *Nostra Aetate*, n.4, the Vatican Guidelines of 1975 and the American Bishops' Guidelines for Catholic-Jewish Relations of 1967.

2.   That homilists and liturgists pay special attention to the presentation and interpretation of scripture so as to promote among the Catholic people a genuine appreciation of the special place of the Jewish people as God's first-chosen in the history of salvation and in no way slight the honor and dignity that is theirs.

3.   That Catholic scholars address themselves in a special way to the theological and scriptural issues raised by those documents which deal with the relationships of the Church with Judaism.

We are firm in our faith that the God of Abraham, Isaac and Jacob and He whom we consider Israel's fairest Son will sustain us in this holy endeavor.

c) EUROPEAN STATEMENTS

Memorandum by the Christian-Jewish Coordinating Committee of Vienna, which served as basis for the Synodal Statement. 1968 (Quoted from Christlich-Pädagogische Blätter, 1968, 2, Vienna. By kind permission. Translated from the German original.)

A legitimate catechetical representation of Judaism is a Christian problem because Christianity without the provisions of the Old Testament is unthinkable or heretical. Christians must try to understand Judaism apart from the terrible consequences of anti-Semitism in recent times. Yet, anti-Semitism frequently operates with religious arguments and it is an important task of Christian catechists to examine those arguments for their justification. Hence, general and practical proposals are herewith submitted for a new version of religious textbooks, as far as they relate to Judaism ....

I. The Unrevoked Covenant

1. A legitimate understanding of the Old Testament, not only from the christological point of view.

The covenant-God of Israel is identical in the Old Testament with the God who made heaven and earth and who preserves them. The very first verse of the Bible indicates this fact.

The making of man was the crowning act of creation. Man was given the particular task to work within and form, creation. Thus Gn 1:28 says: "Then God blessed them and said, 'Be fruitful and multiply. Fill the earth and make it obey you.' " This states the relationship of God to man. As God created the world, man, His image, must responsibly cooperate in the formation of the world (cf. Ps 8).

Contrary to other religions of its time, the Old Testament knows that the evils of the world do not mainly emanate from the gods but are decisively caused by men. The representation in Gn 2 and 3, of the creation, paradise, and sin is an existential answer to the question on the origin of evil: You are guilty yourself. The Hebrew word *adam* means "man", and the Hebrew word *chava* (—Eve) means "life," in the sense of the mother-principle. According to the author of the biblical texts, all human beings, wherever and whenever they live, are prefigured in Adam and Eve. The cause of death and sin, a universal human experience, is traced back to human failure.

In the Old Testament, history is dependent on the obedience of the covenant-people Israel that stands for all mankind; history leads to salvation at the end of time, it is salvation history. God chose this people for absolute obedience. Whenever the people refuses to obey, God directs history in such a way that He punishes His people through other nations (Lv 26:25; Is 7:9; 10:5-7; 47:6f; Hab 1:6; Zach 1:15; etc.). Whenever the people turns to God, He summons a deliverer (cf. Rt; and particularly Is 44:28-45; Ez 33 and 34).

God created the world and all mankind. Noah is seen as the father of all human beings after the Flood, and all the nations are linked to him in salvation history. A covenant was made with Noah (Gn 9) that is valid for all men. From one of the families of Noah's descendants, God elected the patriarchs — Abraham, Isaac, and Jacob — as conveyors of further promises, and with them again He concluded covenants. The patriarchs of Israel, therefore, represent all men, for in Abraham *all* the nations of the earth are to be blessed (Gn 12:3). The covenant with the patriarchs becomes a covenant with the people Israel at Mt. Sinai.

Yet, the Old Testament knows that only a part of the people fulfills the obligations of the covenant. The prophets, therefore, speak of a "remnant" of Israel (Is 37:32; 46:3; Jr 23:3; Am 5:15; Mic 2:12; etc.) that remains true to God, thus representing all of Israel. Just as this remnant stands to the other members of Israel who do not take seriously their obligations towards God, "all Israel" stands with regard to the other nations. Israel, so to speak, is the remnant of the nations. The Old Testament, then, was first to recognize the relationship of God to the world and to man and, because of man's reponsibility, human failure was comprehended as sin.

The prophets already had re-interpreted in a completely personal, moral, existential way the magical, ritualistic concept of sin (cf. Is 6:5) which prevailed in the antique world. That re-interpretation corresponds to a similar change in the biblical concept of God. He must not be represented in image or form (Ex 20:4) and cannot be magically manipulated. The divine Name, "I am who I am" (Ex 3:14) can also be translated, "I shall be who I shall be", that is, I cannot be reached by you or modified by magical practices but I will intervene whenever I wish to do so.

Observance of His law is the heart of obedience to God. Right from the beginning, covenants are linked to covenant-laws, thus the covenant with Noah (Gn 9:3-4) demands abstention from asphyxiated and the Sinaitic covenant has the Decalogue (Ex 20; cf. Pss 1 and 119).

It is part of Israel's election as people of God that it was given the promises (Rom 9 - 11; Gal 3:6-14), which leads to the question of hope for salvation and the messiah, at the end of time.

2. Christological understanding of the Old Testament

The Old Testament awaits universal salvation at the end of time (Is 11:1-10; Ez 36). This expectation is either linked to a messiah or will be realized directly by God, as e.g. in Is 43:16-21.

Hope for a messiah is mainly based on the Davidic kingship ideology of

Jerusalem. His universal reign over all enemies, his enthronement at the right hand of God, and a divine sonship in an adoptive sense, are parts of this ideology (2 Sam 7; Pss 2 and 110 and other coronation psalms). The original expectation was for a real descendant of David but eventually it became the hope for an ideal ruler from the house of David, at the end of time. This kingship ideology took on full messianic character when a reigning issue of David no longer existed, i.e. after the 6th cent. B.C. There is evidence also for the expectation of an eschatological, universal ruler outside of the kingship ideology, e.g. in Nm 24:17, that is, at a very early biblical time.

The Hebrew word *mashiah* (the anointed) also means the enthroned king of the house of David who, as the Anointed of Yahweh, is His representative on earth. In the Old Testament, these words are not used for the messiah; only when the kingship ideas were transferred to eschatological categories, did "messiah" take on this secondary meaning. By the 6th cent. B.C., "messiah" is Ps 2:7 and 1 Sam 2:10 was given an eschatological meaning. The Old Testament speaks of the "crumbling hut of David that must be rebuilt" (Am 9:11f), of a "new David" (Hos 3:4f, Jr 30:9), of a "scion of David" (Jr 23:5f; 33:15f; Zach 3:8; 6:12), or of a messianic "prince" (Ez 34:23f; 37:24-26; cf. Acts 5:31). The specialized term messiah does not come into use before the texts of the intertestamental period. Neither in the Old Testament nor in later Judaism is this representative a savior in the meaning of the New Testament Christ.

The Gospels often use the words son of David or son of man. The idea of the son-of-man-messiah derives from Dan 7:13f; it is even more pronounced in the apocryphal Ethiopian Book of Henoch, chapters 37-71, of about the first cent. B.C. According to these sources, the son of man was from the beginning; or he is Henoch, ascended to heaven, the light of the nations and hope of those who are saddened. He also carries out the last judgment and seats himself on the throne of the glory of God. This concept of the son of man later entered the New Testament.

Prophetic and priestly elements form further aspects of the messiah idea (cf. Hebr. 1:1-11; 7:14-16 for a distinct summary). The Old Testament beginnings for the concept of a new prophet are Moses (Dt 18:15.18), the expectation of the return of Elija (Mal 3:23f) or, generally speaking, the expectation of a true prophet at the end of time (1 Macc 4:46; 14:41; cf. Mk 8:28).

Before Jr 31:31 already, the changed situation is understood as a new covenant, based on the notion that the covenant must be renewed at the end of time because of Israel's ever recurring sinfulness. In that sense, some Jewish groups at the time of Jesus, e.g. the Essenes of Qumran, considered themselves as living under a new covenant.

The appearances of the Risen One as well as faith in Christ's Resurrection made the Old Testament transparent to the Christian witnesses, in a manner quite different from Jewish interpretation, then and in our time. It became apparent that the Life, Passion, and Resurrection of Christ could and must be understood "according to the Scriptures." The New Testament writers knew that, without this foretold faith in the Risen One, their scriptural proofs would not be convincing (Lk 24:13-32; Acts 8:26-40). Beginning with that time, however, the Old Testament could be explained as pointing toward the future Messiah, Jesus of Nazareth.

In the history of religion, the messianic hope developed from unassuming beginnings (Gn 49:10; Nm 24:17) towards an ever greater urgency and distinctness. This corresponds to the Christian interpretation of messianic hope gaining ever more clarity toward fulfillment in Jesus of Nazareth. Beginning with the 6th cent. B.C., older prophetic texts were often "updated" by prophets unknown to us by name, who introduced clearly messianic passages.

Apart from the messiah, Old Testament eschatology knows the concept of a "new creation" by Yahveh, the covenant-God (Is 43:19), and a complete renewal of heaven and earth (Is 65:17; 66:22), which includes the dead, and developed into the hope for resurrection of all flesh (Is 25:8 26:19; Dan 12:2).

3. Salvation comes from the Jews

In the context of *Nostra Aetate* ...., the ecumenical aspect of the dialogue with the Jews must be emphasized. What we have in common with Israel is not only worship of the same covenant-God but acceptance of the Old Testment revelation. Christianity's roots in the Ancient Covenant is the most important mutual bond.

4. Presentation of Judaism in the New Testament age

New Testament writers developed their picture of Judaism from polemic arguments with contemporary Jewish groups. Hence, the latter must be presented as they understood themselves. Judaism at the time of Jesus must on no account be described as a uniform, monolithic bloc.

The Pharisees were the most important group; through obedience of the divine law, they wanted to develop a province of God on earth. In that sense, they saw themselves as the remnant of Israel on whom it depended whether redemption was hastened or delayed. For that reason, the Pharisees, despite their generally liberal views (Acts 5:34-39), were particularly sceptical of all messianic movements at the time of Jesus.

According to the Pharisees, the law of Moses corresponds intellectually to the law of nature and of the world, by which God governed Himself at the Creation. For this and other reasons, the Pharisees held that it was necessary for salvation to fulfill this law with utmost accuracy; they considered those as sinners who lived in indifference of the law. The Old Testament beginnings of such an interpretation are in Gn 2:2-3; God Himself rested on the sabbath, that is why the commandment of the sabbath rest is part of the order of creation, willed by God.

The Sadducees, also mentioned in the New Testament, consisted of the priestly aristocracy and other highly placed and propertied persons. They denied many of the ideas propagated as binding by the Pharisees, e.g. resurrection and the doctrine of angels and demons (cf. Acts 23:6-10). Until the Jewish revolt against Rome in 66 A.D., all the leaders of the Sanhedrin were probably priests, i.e. Sadducees. At the time of writing of the New Testament, neither the Pharisees nor the Sadducees believed in an early appearance of the messiah. That expectation had its home in conventicles who, either by a law-abiding and ascetic life, prepared for an apocalyptic war of revenge against their enemies and those of God (e.g. the Essenes of Qumran), or who believed that, by political activities and force of arms, they had to hasten this holy apocalyptic war (namely, the revolting groups of the Jewish war against Rome, 66-70 A.D., i.e. the Sicarii and Zealots). Those who "waited for the kingdom of God" frequently believed that God demanded hatred of enemy, an idea unknown to Pharisees and Sadducees. It is against those groups, then — not against Pharisees and Sadducees — that Jesus directed His polemic in Mt 5:43f.

Only Pharisees and Sadducees sat in the Sanhedrin, the highest inner-Jewish authority. In the Gospel tradition, the significant discussions of the historical Jesus and the early Jewish-Christian communities took place with representatives of the Sanhedrin, and not with other groups. For that reason, only Pharisees and Sadducees are mentioned. Yet, Mt 5:32f, for instance, indicates that the Jesus tradition contains polemics against other groups as well (e.g. the Qumran Essenes). Mt 26:52-54 is most probably a polemic against the Zealots.

5. *Legitimate historical presentation of Judaism, up to our time.*

Following Mt 27:25, some Christian catechists may feel justified in explaining the post-biblical history of the Jews as if they were permanently accursed because of their rejection of Christ and His crucifixion. This is clearly and definitely contradicted by *Nostra Aetate.*

While in pagan antiquity the Jews were mainly a group living under different laws, they became one of diminished privileges when Christianity became an official religion. Since the era of Constantine, Christianity had to replace the bankrupt emperor cult as an over-arching idea. The Jews, therefore, appeared as nothing more than petrified witnesses to a faith that was no longer topical, they were tolerated for this witness alone. Their inferior legal position within late antiquity and medieval society was seen as proof for the divinity of the messiah rejected by the Jews. This resulted in the prohibition for Jews to hold positions in authority over Christians, which made the former social outsiders in a society based mainly on feudal dependency. In the course of centuries, the tendency of Jews to form communities of their own developed into the formation of ghettos forced upon them from the outside. Jews were believed capable of all kinds of crime, such as ritual murder, desecration of hosts, well-poisoning, etc. A number of popes took position against these accusations in papal bulls, but with little success.

Such accusations became prevalent in the 13th cent. To protect the Jews against arbitrary attacks, they were made "personal servants," i.e. protégés, of the imperial exchequer; as such, they could be loaned or given away to local barons in payment of debts. With few exceptions — e.g. Bernard of Clairvaux, Hildegard of Bingen, Johannes Reuchlin, *et al* — the Jews found little sympathy in late medieval society. Christians were onlookers when Jews who refused forced baptism were burned and murdered in other ways, as were witches and heretics. Jews considered such a martyr's death a witnessing to the God of the covenant and promises, they called it "sanctification of God."

The racism of modern anti-Semitism which developed during the 19th century is inexcusable from a Christian point of view. This applies even where arguments for its justification are borrowed from Christianity. It is anti-Christian and its outbreaks and effects are condemned by the Church.

6.   What positive effect does a legitimate knowledge of Judaism have on Christian catechesis?

Mindful of the fact that Old Testament messianic hope refers to a temporal-eschatological messiah in power and glory but not to one who is to suffer and rise (not even in Is 52:13 - 53:12), we must understand the profound experience of the earliest Jewish Christians, on hearing the message, "Christ is risen and we are His witnesses." The fact alone that, after the external fiasco of Golgotha, His followers did not disperse but kept faith with their unconventional messiah Jesus, is an indication of the powerful influence of their encounter with the Risen One. We Christians must understand as historical justification of our faith, the circumstance that they were Jews who, after Golgotha, proclaimed the Crucified as the Risen One, because resurrection had not previously formed an element of their messianic concept and the cross was but a mark of scandal. We would deny ourselves this justification, were we to reduce to narrow-mindedness and stubbornness the refusal of Jews to believe in the gospel of the Resurrection of Jesus. In our discussions of the Resurrection, Christians can profit from a full and accurate presentation of Old Testament and post-biblical Judaism.

7.   How does the new picture of the Jews relate to recent Christian self-understanding?

The Statement on the Jews can be fully grasped only within the context of Vatican II as a whole, in particular, together with the Constitution On Revelation. The latter refers to the historical development and dependence of the various biblical passages; their meaning beyond that historical setting must be discovered in each case. Under these provisions, the negative statements about the Jews become less important than previously maintained.

The modern Church thinks in ecumenical categories and holds that, though representing and proclaiming the word of God and dispensing the Sacraments, she is still awaiting the full realization of the Kingdom (*adveniat regnum tuum*; Rom 8). Serious theological study of Judaism will prevent that Christians lose sight of their own eschatological expectation.

II. Christian Self-Contradiction

1. From polemics within Judaism towards Christian polemics against the Jews.

The antique world revered the gods but not the One God who created the world. That led to a contrast between pagan religiosity and Jewish monotheism. From the pagan point of view, the Jews were godless because they had no visible gods. The God of Israel must not be portrayed in any form, which was unintelligible to the pagans who erected many resplendent sculptures for their gods. They believed that Israel's god must have the shape of an ass or something similar, which made them hide this god from view.

The law of Israel firmly linked the various Jewish communities of the diaspora. That which made them one, however, separated them from their pagan environment. Jews who kept faith with God and His law could not participate in the life of the pagans, which even within the private sphere was dominated by religious considerations. For that reason, Jews were often accused of being hostile toward anything they were not familiar with.

While the antique gods of various geographical areas were often combined (syncretism), the God of Israel resisted such endeavors. That, too, increased anti-Jewish feelings among the pagans. Old Testament books from 500-100 B.C. (e.g. the Books of Esther, Daniel, and Maccabees 1 and 2) tell of such arguments between believing Jews and their pagan neighbors. The Maccabean revolt of 168-164 B.C. was directed against an attempt by the Syrian king Antiochus IV (he called himself Epiphanus, the visible God) to identify the God of Israel as the Syrian god Baal. It must be considered a tragedy that precisely those strengths and characteristics which enabled Judaism to exist and survive within a pagan environment, resulted in their inability to recognize Jesus of Nazareth as messiah.

The apostles who proclaimed the Messiah Jesus of Nazareth were Jews, as were at first those to whom they brought the Gospel. The polemic tone of the discussions between the Jewish followers of Christ and those who refused to believe in Him is quite noticeable in the Gospel literature.

Existing animosity against the Jews originating in a pagan environment, caused Gentile Christians to interpret polemics among Jews on the messiahship of Jesus as justification for their rejection of Judaism. In that way, Jesus' outcries against the Pharisees and other polemic sayings against contemporary Jewish groups became the foundation for many centuries, of Christian anti-Jewish polemics. Thus already in the Gospel of

John, the Jews became the representatives of those who refused to accept the message of Christ.

Christianity took over from the Old Testament, among other things, the claim to absolutism and applied it not only against the pagans but the people of the Old Testament. A combination of the pagan anti-Jewish disposition and genuine Old Testament postulates produced that intensification of anti-Jewish polemics which marked the relationship between Christians and Jews for many centuries.

Christian opposition to the Jews increased even more when the Jewish question, how the world was changed by the death and resurrection of Christ, was countered with the notion that Jewish refusal to accept Him had prevented the coming of salvation.

The Jews, then, appeared as representatives not only of an antiquated but evil world order, which caused the author of the Apocalypse of John to speak of the "synagogue of Satan" (3:9), a term still in use in anti-Semitic literature which passes itself off as religiously inspired.

2. Polemic as a literary genre

We can correctly interpret the harsh anti-Jewish passages in the New Testament only when we understand their literary style. Our reasoning would cease to be within the meaning of the Scriptures, were we to see such statements as having absolute value instead of setting them against the polemical situation in which they were uttered.

A literary genre is the form and manner of speaking, characteristic for the way in which ideas and emotions at a given time and by people of a given background are rendered. Thus, the outcries over the Pharisees in Mt 23:13-35 presuppose the situation as the Christian messengers of faith first appeared in the synagogues where they could be disciplined (scourged) according to Jewish jurisdiction and from where they could be officially excluded.

The sevenfold "Woe" against the Pharisees culminates in an accusation against the people of prophet-murderers. The controversy goes so far as to make the Pharisees answerable for "all the just blood ever shed on earth, beginning with the blood of Abel" (Mt 23:25). Yet, Matthew knew that Cain, the murderer of his brother, was not a Jew. This polemic barb, then, should make us understand that only Jews in the concrete historical situation of Mt. 25:35 could have been meant, where they represented the persecutors of the Christian Gospel messengers.

Matthew borrowed from the Old Testament prophetic reprimands his harshness of expression as well as the trend for schematization, a trend intensified among those groups from whom the Jewish-Christian communities probably developed. The Qumran Essenes e.g. called the Pharisees "hypocrites", a word eventually used by the author of Dan 11:34 against the Maccabees. Rabbinic Judaism, too, developed a considerable polemic in the Talmud, directed against the enemies of Pharisaism.

Similarly, according to *Nostra Aetate,* Mt 27:25 must not be interpreted as if Jews everywhere and of all times were responsible for the condemnation of Jesus. Matthew's polemical tendency, caused by his anger over the rejection by most Jews of his faith in Christ, cannot be binding as having significance beyond the concrete situation. Mt 27:25 is paradigmatic for a situation in which the Church — as was done in *Nostra Aetate* — must intervene to separate what is important for our faith from what is a mere by-product of contemporary controversies.

Isolating Mt 27:25 from its New Testament context as a whole, would contradict the words of St. Peter in Acts 3:17 where it says that the Jews and their leaders acted in ignorance, hence without malice; such a splitting off would also totally contradict Lk 23:34 and 1 Cor 15:3.

It would be quite wrong to apply controversial sayings of the Bible only to other people. What at that time was spoken against one or another Jewish group, may in our time refer to ourselves. We would miss the pastoral aspect of Mt 23, were we to apply it merely to Jewish imperfections at that time instead of to Christian failure in our own.

III Practical hints for catechists

1. Jesus of Nazareth, the Messiah

    a) Why did and do Jews not accept Him as messiah although they are familiar with the Old Testament?

Jews await a messiah who will reign in a universal kingdom of peace and salvation. Old Testament messianic ideas are quite varied. The messiah is described either as temporal-eschatological king on the throne of David or as heavenly son of man. Essential to the Jewish idea of the messianic kingdom is that it brings to an end all infirmities of this world, namely suffering, oppression, injustice, want, at times even death.

Some parts of Jewish tradition distinguish between a more this-worldly messianic kingdom and a world more defined by the hereafter. This becomes evident in the millenium of the Apocalypse of John, chapter 20. At the beginning, only the just will rise; towards the end, there will be a universal resurrection, ending with the last judgment. Jews did not think that these expectations were fulfilled by the coming of Jesus.

Jesus, however, proved to be a master of demons, He performed miraculous healings and forgave sins. That is why Jews asked why Jesus, who had power over sickness and death, did not use His faculties to bring about final salvation, for which they fervently longed. They could not understand why He mainly employed His power to prove His authority over that of Moses (e.g. Mk 3:1-6). Some became convinced, therefore, that Jesus cast out demons with the help of Beelzebub, while we confess that it was done by the finger of God (Lk 11:14-23).

    b) Why do we believe that Jesus is the messiah and interpret His life, suffering, and resurrection as prefigured in the Old Testament?

The apostolic witness of the Resurrection is authentic. Apart from the Gospel testimonies, it is contained in 1 Cor 15:3-8, postulated in Acts 1:21-22 and, in its probably oldest form, given in Lk 24:34.

In the light of Easter, the early Church gave Jesus the title of Messiah-Christ who, after His Resurrection, was progressively freed from any ambiguity of temporal glory. The Old Testament messianic passages were then applied to Christ who fulfilled them in His life, suffering, and resurrection (cf. Lk 24:13-34). The Church, therefore, understands the Old Testament sayings in the light of a revelation founded on the words and history of Jesus and legitimized after His Resurrection. Enlightened by grace, it is quite legitimate for us Christians to apply to Christ the Old Testament messianic passages.

2. Your Kingdom Come

Based on the Old Testament expectation of universal salvation (cf. particularly Is 11:1-10; Ez 36), Jews are still awaiting the realization of the absolute and visible reign of God. That expectation stirred the early Christians, too (Mk 9:1; 13:28-32; 1 Cor 15:51; 16:22; 1 Thess 4:13 - 5:2).

The evangelists Luke and John in particular, recognized that the elevation and glorification of the Risen Christ was a realization of the Kingdom of God (compare Lk 22:69 with Mk 14:62 and Mt 26:64; Jn 11:17). While the early Church prayed *maranatha*, "come o Lord" (1 Cor 16:22, cf. Acts 22:20; also Didache 10:6), thus asking for the coming of universal salvation, the Gentile Christian Tertullian said about 200 A.D.: "We pray for the emperor, for those in imperial offices, for the continuation of the world, peace for the nations, for the postponement of the end of the world" (*Apolog.* 39.2).

Though movements within the Church persisted, wanting to force the coming of the Kingdom, such expectation gradually retreated in the perception of most Christians. Serious consideration of the question posed by Jews, "what has actually changed since Golgotha and Easter?", will protect us against a superficial interpretation of the prayer, "Your Kingdom come."

Our answer must be that of the apostle Paul who, as a Jew, had to contend with this essentially Jewish question. The law of Moses alone cannot lead to justification (Gal 3) because it does not stand outside of the sinful world. Alone, the Resurrection of Christ and the sending out of the Spirit overcame the present order of suffering and death. A Christian's life, therefore, becomes relevant by baptismal grace for the universal redemption still to come (Rom 8). The definite path to full and universal salvation, then, can lead only, "through Him, and with Him, and in Him" (cf 1 Cor 8:6; Col 1:16-18).

3. The Pharisees

a) What did the Pharisees think of God and man?

God is the Creator of heaven and earth, Lord over life and death, He plans and foresees everything, yet man is given full freedom of will. Death is not the final event for man; there is life after death for the individual as well as a universal resurrection (Acts 23:6-10). God wants salvation for man, but He asks that man prove himself worthy. To this end, moral conduct is sufficient for non-Jews but Jews must persevere in the law given by Moses.

b) What did the Pharisees think of the Mosaic law?

The law of Moses corresponds to the divine order of creation, it is the deposit of this order intended for man. That is why fulfilment of the law leads to salvation, while its neglect delays salvation. The law must never be applied against man and his natural interests. Ministration to a harmless sickness was prohibited on the sabbath, but dangerous illness could be healed, just as other acts prohibited on the sabbath were permitted as soon as it was a question of saving a life. Jesus' healing of an illness that did not endanger life, therefore, was a provocation to the Pharisees (Mk 3:1-6).

c) What did the Pharisees think about the messiah?

About the middle of the 2nd cent. B.C., Pharisaism arose as a religio-political group that denied the widely accepted early expectation of the messiah (as well as the apocalyptic dualism that was part of it). Pharisees believed that the coming of the messiah cannot be forced and that the time of his coming cannot be calculated in advance. That separated them not only from Christianity but from other Jewish groups who expected the coming of the kingdom (Apocalyptics and Zealots). Despite their suspicions against all those who expected the imminent approach of or already realized messianic time (Apocalyptics and Christians), the Pharisees, too, knew that at some undefined point in time the rule of the son of David would begin.

d) Why do the Gospels represent the Pharisees in such negative light?

The Pharisees realized that the law of Moses in its original version could not be uniformly applied to the events of the changing times, but must be constantly adapted. Such an accommodation they attempted by an interpretation of the law, while the apocalyptic groups accepted an authoritative version (cf. on the lips of Jesus: "But I say to you .....") We must also consider that it was quite common in the Old Testament to use polemic subtleties, which influenced New Testament sayings about the Pharisees.

The heated arguments of Jesus against the Pharisees must be explained by the fact that the Gospel tradition developed in opposition to the Pharisees.

4.   The process against Jesus and His Passion

The Marcan Text, as the oldest Gospel, should be used. Parallel traditions should be mentioned and presented in their polemical and historical context, according to the students' age. We must never speak of a one-sided guilt of Jews in the Cross of Christ, nor must the Cross be interpreted as consequence of the blindness or ill-will of the Jewish leaders.

We must refer to the concrete legàl situation in the Roman province of Judea, according to which the Jews were not empowered to impose the death penalty (Jn 18:31). We do not pray in the Creed, "suffered under the high priest Caiaphas," but "suffered under Pontius Pilate." Acts 2:23-3:17 must be mentioned, where St. Paul says to his Jewish fellow citizens: "I know that you have acted in ignorance, as have your leaders." Speaking of the Crucifixion, Lk 23:34 must be referred to: "Forgive them, Father, for they know not what they do."

Discussing the redemptive meaning of the Passion, we must not forget that Jesus did not die for the sins of the Jews but for the sins of all men. We must prevent by all means that the problem of guilt develops into an accusation by (sinful) Christians against (also sinful) Jews.

Abraham's faith, offered in complete trust, was rendered in the name of all who believe in God, while Caiaphas refused to believe as a representative of all sceptics. Belief and unbelief, thus, presuppose a divine claim on man that becomes intelligible only by Jewish acceptance of the Covenant. What we, on the basis of Christianity, call Jewish unbelief must be seen in the context of God's Covenant with Israel and His promises to them. It was out of His love that God made His Covenant with Israel, just as Christ died and rose again, out of love, that we may die and rise with Him (Jn 11).

The Diocesan Synod of Vienna issued the following Statement (published in: "Leben und Wirken der Kirche in Wien", Handbuch der Synode 1969-1971, pp 235f). With kind permission, translated from the German.

The Church recognizes the Old and the New Testament as divine word and instruction. The New Testament can be comprehended only in the light of the Old Testament. The latter is not simply a preparation for the New Testament but possesses religious importance of its own. The Old Testament's message of salvation must, therefore, be used and interpreted in theological reflection as well as in the religious life of the parishes.

Christians and Jews became witnesses of the living word of God and His work of salvation. Before the world, therefore, they must witness responsibly to the Revelation of God. According to Romans 9 - 11, the existence and history of the Jewish people are mysteries of salvation in the eyes of Christians; hence, the latter must see the existence of the Jews of our day as a part of salvation history.

We firmly believe that the New Covenant in Christ did not abrogate the promises of the Old, as the Apostle said in chapter 11 of his Letter to the Romans (particularly verses 1, 26, 28). All other New Testament passages relating to the Jews must be suitably interpreted in the light of that text. We Christians are not permitted to consider the Jews a people that, though originally elected, was finally rejected by God.

Christians and Jews are united in a common hope for the full revelation of the Kingdom of God. They are equally linked by the idea of man as an image of God, and their endeavor to master the world in the spirit of religion.

More frequent use of Old Testament texts in the new arrangement of liturgical passages should be made, to improve the understanding of the Old Testament by the faithful. A suitable introduction to the often unknown religious background of these texts should be offered. In no case, however, must the Old Testament texts be omitted regularly or on principle.

In the classroom, in textbooks and other teaching material for religious instruction, untrue statements about the Jewish people must not only be avoided but those, apparently negative, statements of Scripture must be explained with reference to pauline theology. The religious content of the Old Testament must be emphasized and the significance of Israel as covenant partner of God presented positively.

Study of the Old Testament during the period of theological formation and an exegetical understanding gained thereby, should lead to a more frequent use of the Old Testament in preaching, catechesis, and liturgy. Common study, as recommended by *Nostra Aetate,* could be realized by guest presentations of Jewish theologians at theological departments, as well as by more intensified Judaistic studies by theological students. It is recommended that institutes for Catholic adult education deal more intensively with the topics "Old Testament" and "Judaism." Those in charge should urge the faithful to own a complete copy of the Scriptures.

The psalms as biblical prayer texts should not be repressed in church services or diocesan hymnals and prayer books. The faithful should thereby become better acquainted with Old Testament texts.

It is contrary to the doctrine of Christ's Church to interpret the suffering and humiliations inflicted upon the Jews by Christians and Non-Christians over many centuries, as a consequence of their rejection by God. Christians, therefore, must keep free from anti-Jewish affects and oppose anti-Semitic discrimination by others. The Church of Vienna expects that Catholics leave nothing undone to overcome the present estrangement between Christians and Jews, which was fed by traditional misunderstanding.

During the Plenary Session of the Pastoral Council of the
Catholic Church in the Netherlands in 1970 at Noordwijkerhout, a
series of "Pastoral Recommendations" were studied from a plan for
"Relations between Jews and Christians." This final document was
drawn up by the Sub-Commission "The Church and Israel".
According to the methods of this Pastoral Council, only the "Pastoral
Recommendations" were voted on and are now official conclusions.
(Quoted in SIDIC, Vol. III No. 2, 1970). With kind permission.

Plan of report: "Relations between Jews and Christians"
Introduction — Motives and plan

The Pastoral Council of the Roman Catholic Church in the Netherlands considers it desirable to examine her attitude towards the Jewish people.[1]

1. The Jews have made important contributions to the history of Dutch civilization, and the Netherlands have played a prominent role in Jewish life and thought during past centuries, so that our capital has been called the Jerusalem of the West.

2. The destruction of most of the Jewish communities in the Netherlands in the horrifying persecution during the years of occupation — 1940-1945 — still calls for reflection: on the one hand to uphold the living remembrance of the courage and faith-inspired power which were demonstrated by so many in privation and under torture; and, on the other hand, it must not be forgotten that many Christians failed in their duty as a consequence of centuries of Christian anti-Semitism, which has been used as a warning by the Provincial Council of the Dutch Roman Catholic Church.[2]

1. The expression "Jewish people" immediately raises the question of the exact significance of this term. We take our stand from the conviction expressed in the Old Testament and confirmed in the New, that the Jewish people has an existence specifically its own. Its existence as a people (its origin and centuries of vicissitudes), however, display characteristics which place it outside of ordinary categories. This is why it is impossible to define the expression "Jewish people". They have never been able themselves to find a solution acceptable to all, and this report does not attempt to do so either. The title "Jewish people" was preferred to "Jews" because the latter suggests that the individual Jew is different from other men, whereas it is solely their particular existence as a *people* with which this document is concerned. The name "Jews", moreover, fails to recognize the solidarity of the Jewish people, dispersed as they are throughout the whole world. The name "Israel" is also avoided because of its divergent overtones, even more acute than those of "Jewish people". This document wishes to be an expression only of relations between Jews and Christians as such, insofar as they belong to the Jewish people or the Christian community. As the Jewish people is not simply a religious group, its existence among other nations always has political implications. This report bears no judgment on such implications, even where they touch on such aspects as the internationalization of Jerusalem or the administration of the Holy Places.

2. *Acta et decreta concilii provincialis ultrajectensis* 1924, canon 1325, par. 3, p. 183: "Relations with Jews must be avoided because this people is very estranged from the doctrine of the Cross of Christ, a scandalous thing for them. Parish priests must take care that Christians do not work for Jews who would use them as servants or subordinates. If there is no danger of faith or morals, paid daily work may be undertaken for Jews, either in agriculture or in factories. A grave warning is given, however: such services must not lead to others which would endanger the soul, arising above all from a desire for lucre. Moreover, the faithful must take care—according to the warning of Benedict XIV (Enc. *A quo primum,* 1751),—never to need the help or support of Jews."

3.   The Jewish people have their special place in the Church's faith. They can never be simply equated with non-Christian peoples. The Church knows that she cannot be the Church for all Nations, without being connected to the living Jewish people of today. She believes that, through her Head, Jesus Christ, she remains united for ever to the Jewish people, not only historically, but also in its continued existence. The unbroken and particular link between the Jewish people and the Church must be a determining factor in the Church's own mission, and her attitude towards the present-day Jewish people. This will help the Church to a better understanding of her mission in the world, and to the fostering of unity with other Churches.

Only a few problems have been treated here from among the many that exist in Jewish-Christian relations. The report tries to avoid looking upon relations with the Jewish people exclusively from biblical and theological data, and neglecting the development of Jewish life after the year AD 70 (and 130).

It is a speciality of the spirit of Judaism to learn from the day-to-day lessons of history. That is why the starting point of the relationship is the attitude towards the Jews throughout the centuries. And, in virtue of biblical, historical, and theological data, some principles have been formulated which should determine relations between Jews and Christians.

The close connection between Jews and Christians consists not only in the historical origin of Christianity in Judaism but, above all, despite different outlooks, they have many elements in common in the Church's daily life, and in Jewish worship, namely: the liturgy of the Word, the Lamb of God and the ministry of reconciliation. For this reason a special paragraph has been devoted to this point.

Attention is also called to the improvement in social relations between Jews and Christians, in two paragraphs, Catechesis concerning the Jewish people, and Education and Information regarding the relations between Jews and Christians.

Chapter 1 Anti-Semitism
Referring to the Declaration of Vatican II *Nostra Aetate,* the Pastoral Council condemns every form of anti-Semitism.

1.   The Vatican Council states (*Nostra Aetate,* No. 5): "We cannot in truthfulness call upon that God who is the Father of all, if we refuse to act in a brotherly way towards all men, created as they are in God's image. A man's relationship to God the Father and his relationship with his brother men are so linked together that Scripture says: 'He who does not love, does not know God' (1 Jn 4:8). This is a condemnation of any theory or practice which discriminates between one man and another, between one people and another, in their human dignity, hence in their human rights."
2.   This is particularly true in any sincere reflection about relations with Jews and with the Jewish people. Anti-Semitism is not only a form of unjust

STEPPING STONES TO FURTHER JEWISH-CHRISTIAN RELATIONS

discrimination with regard to a human group or people, but it is also resistance to a fundamental view of life. It is directed not only against the Jews as an ethnic or sociological group but, above all, against their very existence as the result of their history and religious experience. In this context, anti-Semitism fundamentally means a misjudgement of the very nature of God's action with the Jewish people, the firstborn of all peoples. If this aspect of anti-Semitism is not recognized, we continue to risk making a wrong estimation of the qualities and behavior of the Jewish people.

3.   In the past and even today, Christians and their Churches have looked upon the history of God's people too much from their own, all too human, point of view. The Church has always been predominantly considered the Church of the Gentiles, to the exclusion of the Jewish people, and a common spiritual heritage has been lost. This, among other things, has been the cause of unspeakable injustices that have been committed against the Jews. The extent of such injustice was revealed in this present century, when the vast number of Christians and their Churches hardly raised their voices against a massacre of the Jewish people which exceeds all imagining — a massacre in which all men share responsibility.

4.   Religious thinking about the very existence of the Jewish people as such shows that there is a particular relationship between the Jewish people and the Promised Land. The Jews consider this relationship not only as historical, cultural, or religious phenomenon but as an indissoluble element in their expectation of the day when all nations will embrace in peace and justice. To neglect or deny this fact may be the cause of misunderstanding and help to nourish prejudice about the nature of the Jewish people and its place among the nations, a misunderstanding which has already led and may lead again to discrimination. The presence of anti-Semitism requires great caution and a sound knowledge of Jewish reality.

Chapter II The Relationship of the Church to the Jewish people

The Declaration of the Second Vatican Council indicates the spiritual connection of the people of the New Testament with that of Abraham's race (*Nostra Aetate,* No.4a). The Council points out the continuation of the Old Testament in the New, and how the Church was prefigured and took root in the Jewish people. In his Letters to the Ephesians and Romans, St. Paul recalled the connection which has always existed between the Church and the Jewish people; the great spiritual patrimony which they share, and how the Church, together with the prophets and the same Apostle, awaits the day, known to God alone, when all nations will invoke the Lord "and serve him with one consent" (Zeph 3:9).

The Pastoral Council of the Roman Catholic Church in the Netherlands believes that, according to the Law, the Prophets and the Psalms (Lk 24:44; Lk 13:34-35), the Jewish people has been constituted for ever as a testimony of God's saving alliance with mankind (Is 43:10; Rm 9-11). God's promise *par excellence* to the Jewish people is the everlasting covenant (cf Rm 9:4-5; 11:29; Eph 2:12). The Pastoral Council believes that Jesus Christ, born under the Law (cf Gal 4:5), is the one whom the prophets, the righteous and kings desired to see (Mt 13:17; Lk 10:24), because in Him the revelation of God's eternal love reached its plenitude (cf Eph 1:10; Col 1:15-23). The Pastoral Council states that in Jesus Christ, peace has been initiated, uniting the two worlds and breaking down the wall of separation between Jews and Gentiles (cf Eph 2:14-15). He shall come to complete this peace (Jn 16:33; Rev 21). That is why also the as yet unfulfilled promises of God to the Jewish people are held in honor in liturgical prayer.

With gratitude the Roman Catholic Church in the Netherlands commemorates the true spiritual tradition in which the Jews have preserved the Law and the Prophets. She also recognizes the many spiritual and religious values existing among the Jewish people, which provide a permanent stimulus and the reason for an examination of the Church's conscience, being as they are of great significance for justice and peace in the whole world.

Consequently, the Roman Catholic Church in the Netherlands is doing her utmost to promote the renewal of Jewish-Christian relations through mutual knowledge and esteem, as the Second Vatican Council proposed to the whole Church. Searching the Scriptures and history together with equal readiness to learn from them will be a great contribution to this cause. Any intention or design for proselytism must be rejected as contrary to human dignity and Christian conviction. Moreover, the position of the Jewish people with regard to the universal message of Christ cannot be equated with the position of those professing other non-Christian religions. Christians are confronted today with the problem of recognizing the ways of God in human history, as well as the position of religion in a secularized society. It may be appropriate to attempt an integration of Jewish tradition into our approach to these questions.

Chapter III Relations with the Jewish people in the liturgy
1. The link between the Jewish people and the Church comes to light especially in public worship where it is mysteriously experienced. In word and sacrament, in hymn and prayer, the community celebrates the living Presence of Christ, the Head of His Body in the Spirit. What God has done in His people, Christ consolidated and brought to its ultimate completion by His unique and eternal mediation. In the liturgy, the Church experiences a new creation in Christ, and a participation in Abraham's offspring and Israel's dignity (baptism, liturgy of the Passover night). Christ is "the true Easter Lamb that takes away the sins of the world" (Easter Preface). Partaking of it, we proclaim His death until He comes again.

In the essential elements of her liturgy the Church preserves the heritage of Jewish worship, both in content and form; the proclamation of the word of God, the celebration of the Passover meal, the ministry of reconciliation in baptism, and the sacrament of penitence.

2. Only in the awareness of this bond, will true relations between Jews and Christians come about. By living and realizing this link, the community of Christ will reach her true stature. This principle formed the original liturgy of the Church, its service of the word and Eucharistic celebration, Advent and Christmas, Passover from Lent to Pentecost, and the entire reconciliation ministry. Liturgical renewal always has to be alive to this idea, in order to maintain the sound proclamation of the ecumenical and eschatological character of the liturgy.

This should draw our attention to the following concrete proposals:

a) Psalms should be used in the liturgy rather than hymns, not only because the Church has always considered the Book of Psalms her book of prayer but in the psalms the proclamation of salvation is put into words in striking and many-faceted ways.

b) The readings, especially those concerning the Jewish people and the Promised Land, should contribute to a correct understanding of the Christian link with the Jewish people.

c) Prayers, especially those of the Eucharistic celebration, must express Christ's love for all men and His love of His own people.

3. All traces of anti-Semitism should disappear. This applies to texts in some parts of the Missal and Breviary, particularly to presentations of Christ's Passion where Jesus, Mary, and the apostles are featured as non-Jews while the other Jews are caricatured. Care must be taken that old prejudices do not unintentionally creep in again.

4. Texts that may give rise to misunderstanding if read out of context or without knowledge of the historical circumstances or linguistic usage of the times, should be carefully placed in their right perspective in all sermons so that they may contribute to a new attitude towards the Jewish people.

Chapter IV Catechesis and the Jewish people

1. Catechesis should provide an important contribution to the improvement of Jewish-Christian relations, and to fruitful interaction between Judaism and Christianity. In the past, it was the way in which catechesis was presented that prejudice was fostered against the Jewish people, in succeeding generations. Even present-day catechesis frequently fails in these respects: mainly by unconscious misjudgment or disdain of the Jewish people, past or present; by lack of a positive approach to the Jewish people; by an insufficient concept of the true nature and extent of anti-Semitism.

2. Conditions to develop a correct catechesis regarding the Jewish people are:

a) A thorough knowledge and a right understanding of the Bible as the proclamation of God's action in mankind. A correct relationship to the Jewish people can never come about as long as the Christian feels a stranger to the Bible. Belittling ideas about the Jewish people will inevitably live on as long as the preaching of Jesus and the apostles is detached from its historical Jewish background and Christianity presented as a system of abstract truths. The history of the Jewish people before and after Christ must be considered in its particular meaning for salvation history.

b) A sincere, faithful reflection on the relationship of the Church to the Jewish people, according to the ideas developed in the previous chapter.

c) Respect for the full historical truth about the Jewish people and correct information on present-day Jews and Judaism.

3. Certain points that demand particular attention:

a) The Jewish people must be seen as the people with whom God concluded His covenant for all time. The Old Testament does not exist only as a prefiguration of the New but has a significance of its own, in Jewish as in world history.

b) The Jewish people is not collectively guilty of the Passion and the Death of Jesus Christ nor of His rejection as Messiah. Though the Jewish authorities and their followers clamored for His death, *Nostra Aetate* (No. 4) states: "... what happened in His Passion cannot be blamed upon all the Jews then living, without distinction, nor upon the Jews of today." The Jewish people is not condemned nor bereft of its election. Their sufferings, dispersion, and persecutions are not punishments for the Crucifixion or rejection of Jesus. It is unjust to accuse the Jews of "deicide."

c) It is not self-evident at all that a complete rupture occurred between Jews and Christians since Jesus Himself — born of a Jewish mother — never severed the bonds with His people. The young Church was rooted in the Jewish people.

d) Catechesis should truthfully represent the religious life of Jews in our day.

e) It is incorrect and unfair to place the New Testament and the Old in opposition to one another, the New Testament as a covenant of love, the Old as one of fear. The proclamation of God's love for man and man's love for his fellow men in charity, fidelity, and justice forms an essential part of the Old Testament.

f) The Gospel message and apostolic preaching about the significance of the Jewish people in the ultimate unification of the world (Mt 23:37-39; Lk 13:35; Acts 1:7; Rom 9-11; Eph 2:11-22) should be brought into more distinctive relief.

Chapter V Education and information

1. All who are responsible for instruction and education should be taught during their training the permanent significance of the Jewish people in God's plan for mankind. The history of persecutions should not be concealed and the Jewish people must not be treated as though non-existent.

2. It is important to develop concrete plans to promote knowledge about Judaism, preferably together with other Churches.

3. In the training of future priests, study of the Jewish people as they understand their own existence is recommended.

4. An appeal is made to the mass media, to promote renewed Jewish-Christian relations.

PASTORAL RECOMMENDATIONS *(Officially voted on and adopted)*

1. That the Catholic Church in the Netherlands be guided by the religious conscience expressed in the Declaration of the Second Vatican Council *Nostra Aetate* No. 4, in her relations with Jews. We recall that:

   a) The Jews remain most dear to God because of the Fathers (Rom 9:4-5; 11:28);

   b) The Church of Christ is grafted on the Jewish people (cf Rom 11:27-24);

   c) There is a spiritual patrimony common to Jews and Christians.

2. The Pastoral Council recognizes that the biblical message came to the Church in and from the Jewish world of thought and faith, therefore,

   a) A thorough knowledge and correct understanding of the Bible as the proclamation of God's way of acting with mankind cannot be fully attained without familiarity with Jewish awareness of God and Jewish understanding of biblical terms;

   b) It should be acknowledged that not only the Old Testament but the New one as well can be reckoned among Jewish writings, and that the New Testament cannot be understood without knowledge of the Jewish background;

   c) Study of the Scriptures by Jews and Christians together is desirable;

   d) It is necessary for the Church that fidelity to the original text of the Scriptures be safeguarded.

3. A common re-orientation on their Jewish origin is necessary for the progress of an encounter between the different Churches.

4. The Pastoral Council rejects all forms of anti-Semitism and declares in particular:

   a) That, in continuation of the Declaration of the Second Vatican Council, it not only deplores but positively condemns all forms of anti-Semitism;

b) It wishes to repeat that the Passion of Christ cannot be blamed on all the Jews then living nor on Jews of today; they should, therefore, not be considered accursed or rejected;

c) That humanitarian grounds alone are sufficient for the condemnation of discrimination against Jews as a special group in world society and followers of a particular religion and concept of life;

d) That the Church has the duty to reflect on the entire history of the Jewish people before and after Christ and on their self-understanding;

e) That a joint study by Jews and Christians on their common origin and the causes of their separation, based on modern Jewish and Christian intellectual developments, is needed;

f) That the Dutch Episcopate should be asked to declare null and void what was said in the *acta et decreta concilii provincialis ultrajectensis* 1924, canon 1325, par. 3, p. 183 (see footnote 2).

5.   The Pastoral Council wants to bear witness that the Catholic Church in the Netherlands jointly with other Christians as well as Jews:

a) wishes to live according to God's promise of justice and peace;

b) wishes to serve the welfare of the whole of creation;

c) wishes to seek the answers to questions about the idea of God, the image of man, the eschatological expectation, as they co-determine the general and religious crises of the West today.

6.   The Pastoral Council emphatically requests those responsible to give constant and serious attention to a deeper penetration of these thoughts, the results of further study, and reflections in theological formation, preaching, catechesis, liturgy, and publications.

National Catholic Commission for Relations between Christians and Jews. Belgium, 1973. Eighteen Theological Theses.
A Study Paper for Purposes of further Research.
("Bijdragen" Amsterdam 37, 1976. Translated from the French.) With kind permission.

The Unity of Divine Revelation
1.   In the Bible, that is, the Old Testament as well as the New, the same living God, Creator, and Author of Salvation, speaks to all of us, and His salvific works concern all mankind. The Old Testament is an unalienable part of Holy Scripture and must have its place in Christian life and thought. While reading the Old Testament in the light of the New, we must also read it in accord with its own characteristics and as an elucidation of the New Testament. The unity of divine revelation and the fact that Christ came to confirm in the New Testament the message of the Old, indicate that one cannot read the one without the other.

2. The eschatological promise of the New Covenant (Jer 31:31-34) contains the inalienable divine promise to restore the people's relationship with God after the Covenant had been broken by human infidelity. The restoration of the Covenant signifies that it is reinstated in its original splendor. The deformation of divine law caused by human infidelity makes necessary its restoration in Christ. It is, then, the same divine Covenant — expression of the will and fidelity of God — which began with Abraham, was confirmed to the Hebrew people at Sinai and restored by Christ.

3. Can we say that Jesus elevated himself above the authority of Moses? Without denying the possibility of disagreement between certain Gospel texts and the message of Jesus, we can affirm that it by no means was Jesus' intention to abolish the Law or the Prophets, but to fulfill them (Mt 5:17). According to the fifth chapter of the Gospel according to St. Matthew, fulfillment of the law of Moses means, first of all, to concretize, define, and apply to everyday life, the general commandments of the Decalogue (5:20-30). The Decalogue is thereby confirmed by Christ. Fulfillment of the Mosaic law henceforth means rejection of certain interpretations of the Law and of obsolete or by tradition wrongly interpreted, commandments (Mt 5:31-48). We can say with St. John that "the law was given through Moses, grace and truth came through Jesus Christ" (Jn 1:17). This affirmation, however, does not imply a contradiction between law and grace; they are two inseparable aspects of divine revelation. Jesus Christ came to confirm the message of the First Covenant, in a unique and definitive, i.e. normative, way. Born of the Jewish people, he clearly lived according to the law of Moses, if somewhat independent of the religious establishment, as was typical of some Jewish groups.

4. Even St. Paul did not want to break with Israel, his people. He underlines that "the gifts and the calling of God are without repentance" (Rom 11:25-29). Paul's statements on the Jewish law must be interpreted in their original context; that means we must try to place them within the polemical discussions about practical aspects of the religious life *(balakha),* discussions within Judaism which were quite lively at that time. Paul likes to contrast the domination and enslavement of the Law to the service of Christ, the dead and cold letter to the renewal in the spirit of Christ. He does not envisage, however, two successive economies of salvation, opposed to and different from, each other by their very nature. He recognizes only one salvific design of God, and Christ as its final consummation (Rom 10:4). First of all Paul, and with him several rabbis of his time (e.g. *Pirke Aboth),* is against a legalistic attitude towards the Torah (=divine instruction, divine revelation). It would be unfair to consider legalism, against which he warned the disciples of Christ, the proper definition of the Judaism of his time.

Paul underlines the new possibilities of a life in Christ. To renew one's self in the spirit of Christ, to live in the law of Christ, means to become free of the dead letter and of legalism *(nomos),* to find in Christ all of the divine

Torah. When Paul compares justification by faith to works of faith (Rom 3:37), it does by no means indicate an abrogation of the Law (cf Rom 3:31). Despite their different views, moreover, there is no contradiction between Paul and James regarding the works of the Law. St. Paul underlines the fact that we are justified by faith in Christ, not by the works of the Law (Rom ch. 3). St. James insists that faith must prove and manifest itself in works, e.g. in the works of the Law (Jas 2:14ff). The idea that the sacrifice of Christ replaces the levitic sacrifices and that Christ is the high priest of a new covenant after the abrogation of the ancient law, is peculiar to the Letter to the Hebrew (ch. 7 and 8). This assertion must be interpreted in its original historical context, that is, nostalgia for the cult among the Jewish-Christian exiles and the final break between Christians and Jews after the destruction of the Temple (70 CE), particularly after the second Jewish revolt (132-135 CE). The theses of the Letter to the Hebrews are a theological justification for the separation of Christianity and Judaism.

5. According to Christian faith, the Kingdom of God was made manifest in the person of Christ. This fact should not let us forget that Christians, in common with Jews, hope in the coming Kingdom of God. This hope supports the actions and prayers of Jews and Christians, particularly their concrete efforts to realize in this world, justice and peace. Christians and Jews, side by side, must bear the tension of the *already* and the *not yet,* of *this* world and the one *to come,* which differentiate their messianic expectations.

Interpretation of NT texts regarding the Jews
6. The preaching of Jesus and his Apostles must not be detached from the background of their Jewish tradition, Palestinian as well as Hellenistic, in the midst of which the faith of the first Christian communities developed. For the study of Judaism at the time of Christ, we must turn to the Jewish sources in order to discover the authentic values they express and to become familiar with the religious climate and life they reflect.

7. Some Gospel passages about the Jews gave rise to wrong and dangerous interpretations. When the Synoptics and St. John employ the collective term "the Jews," they do not mean all the Jews at the time of Christ, and even less so, all those of history. Generally speaking and particularly in the Fourth Gospel, the term means the adversaries of Jesus, comparable to the term "the world." That also applies to the parables: for instance, the elder brother of the prodigal or the murderous vinegrowers are wrongly identified with all the Jewish people. Beyond the lack of faith and the jealousy of his time, Jesus wants to condemn the faithlessness threatening all of us. The mainly negative picture of the Pharisees in the Gospels must be corrected by objective information from rabbinic literature. Jesus' attitude to the forms of ritual purity is a characteristic of his message; yet, we must not infer from it a principle of opposition

between Judaism as "religion of ritual" and Christianity as "religion of the spirit."

8. New Testament passages on the destiny of the Jewish people refer to the tradition of the Prophets of Israel, who to the threat of rejection joined the promise of final restoration.

9. It is obvious that the Jewish people as such is not guilty of the condemnation and death of Jesus Christ in his Passion, nor of the refusal of his Messianic mission. We must not cast suspicion upon the good faith of the Jewish contemporaries of Jesus, regarding their fidelity to Judaism and their opposition to a Christianity in the making. From a theological point of view, moreover, we must underline the solidarity in sin of all mankind. "Christ underwent his passion and death freely, because of the sins of men ...." (*Nostra Aetate,* n. 4).

The Church and the Jewish People

10. To insist that the Church has taken the place of the Jewish people as salvific institution, is a facile interpretation according to which everything new replaces the old. In that sense, the new covenant evokes the idea of an old one, the new people of God that of an old Israel, etc. The eschatological biblical promise of a new covenant means essentially the definitive and decisive restoration of the Covenant after the rupture caused by human infidelity. According to Christian faith, that promise was realized in the Messiah Jesus. The Church may call herself "people of the covenant" only to the extent that she lives — as body of Christ — according to the message and Messianic reality of Jesus. She will not fully be that people until the end of time.

11. The fundamental Christian commandment, promulgated in the Old Testament and confirmed by Jesus Christ, to love God and neighbor, is binding for Christians and Jews in all their human relations and without exception.

12. We must avoid to disparage biblical or post-biblical Judaism, its laws, institutions, and ways of life, for the purpose of elevating Christianity, by misplaced caricaturistic opposites, e.g: legalism-faith; flesh-spirit; fear-love; doctrine-life; earth-heaven; cult-works; institutional sclerosis-prophetic elan; promise-realization. These actually are constructive tensions which exist between communities, and at the heart of any community of a religious order.

13. The Jewish people is a true relative of the Church, not her rival or a minority to be assimilated. The descendants of Abraham and the Christian people must not enter into competition in the history of salvation. In the dialectic of divine grace and human liberty Christians and Jews fulfil their specific roles and stimulate each other regarding the salvation of the nations (Rom ch. 9 - 11).

14. By faith in Christ, who himself had deep roots in Israel, the Christian community has part in the promises made to the people of God. According to Paul, the Church of non-Jews has part in the call and the mission of Israel (Rom 11:16ff: the olive tree and the grafts; Eph 2:19: citizens with the saints).

15. In content as well as form Christian liturgy, the Eucharist in particular, is by its origin closely related to the religious practice of the Jewish people. Christians have learned from Jews to pray the Psalms and the texts of the Scriptures, and to bless God for His gifts. They celebrate in their great Christian festivals the memory of important moments of the Covenant; for Jesus Christ, in the feasts of Easter and Pentecost, has revealed the continuity of the Father's plan of liberation for mankind. Christians will also find riches in the liturgy of the Jewish home and family.

16. Since the relations with Jews are linked to the very mystery of the Church (*Nostra Aetate,* n. 4), all the churches and Christian communities are called upon to promote them. Christian unity cannot be realized without a return to the sources, not only by taking up the relationship at the place where it was broken, but rather by rediscovering the roots of Jesus and his message in the history and tradition of his people. To exclude Judaism as well as the Judaism of our time from Christian source material, would be a misunderstanding of the Jewish origins of Christianity. An approach to Judaism, on the other hand, from the view point of Christian sources, goes hand in hand with profound respect for Judaism's own and different character.

17. The suffering, persecution, and dispersion which Jews had to endure, must not be represented as an inevitable fate or, worse, a punishment. Anti-Semitism in all its forms, the always latent religious anti-Semitism in particular, must be denounced and combatted, in order to be more true to Christian faith and divine revelation; to make possible authentic relations between Christians and Jews; and as a condition for the establishment of a more humane world.

18. To the extent that Christianity rediscovers in Judaism the roots of her own faith and no longer considers Judaism an errant or obsolete religion, the missionary witness of the Church will no more attempt a "conversion of the Jews," in the current sense of the term, that is, annexation or proselytism. Christians have a duty to witness to their faith in Jesus the Messiah, in particular by their works. This witness, however, in order to be true to the message of Christ, must be a message of love, justice, and respect for others. With regard to Judaism in particular, Christian witness must be humble and respectful because it must take into account the common elements of Jewish and Christian Messianic hope.

Statement by the French Bishops' Committee for Relations with Jews. April 1973. Translated from the French.

I. Jewish existence as a problem addressed to the conscience of Christians

The present existence of the Jewish people, its often precarious fate in the course of history, its hopes, the tragic trials it has known in the past and particularly in modern times, and its partial gathering in the land of the Bible; all these realities can enlighten the life of Christians and add to a more profound understanding of their own faith. The continuity through the ages of this people that has survived other civilizations, its presence as a rigorous and exacting partner of Christendom, are facts of great importance that we must not treat with ignorance or contempt. The Church, speaking in the name of Jesus Christ and, through Him, linked to the Jewish people since her beginnings and for all time, perceives in the uninterrupted existence of this people through the centuries a sign that she would wish fully to comprehend.

II. The slow formation of Christian conscience

On October 28, 1965 the Second Vatican Council solemnly promulgated the Declaration *Nostra Aetate,* which contains a chapter on the Jewish people. We reaffirm the importance of this text which recalls that the Church nourishes herself from the roots of the true olive tree onto which the wild branches, i.e. the Gentiles, were grafted. As Episcopal Committee for the Relations with Jews, it is our duty to point out the topical significance of this Declaration and indicate its practical application.

The position taken by the Second Vatican Council should be considered a beginning rather than a final achievement. It marks a turning point in Christian attitudes toward Jews and opens a path, permitting us to take the exact measure of our task. The Council Statement bases itself on a return to Scriptual sources and breaks with the mentality of the past. It calls all Christians to a new vision of the Jewish people, not only on the level of human relations but also on that of faith. It is impossible, of course, to re-examine all at once the assertions and historical attitudes of the Church, maintained for many centuries. Christian conscience has initiated a process, however, to recall the Jewish roots of the Church. It is important that a beginning has been made, that all strata of the Christian people be reached, and that the course be pursued with honesty and energy.

III. The permanent vocation of the Jewish people

We cannot consider the Jewish religion as we would any others now existing in the world. Through the people of Israel, faith in the One God was inscribed on the history of mankind and monotheism became — if even with certain differences — the common good of three great families which claim the heritage of Abraham, Judaism, Christianity, and Islam.

According to biblical revelation, God Himself constituted this people, brought it up, advised it of His plans, concluding with it an eternal Covenant (Gn 17:7), and giving it a vocation which St. Paul qualifies as "irrevokable" (Rom 11:29). We are indebted to the Jewish people for the Five Books of the Law, the Prophets, and the other Scriptures which complete the message. After having been collected by oral and written tradition, these precepts were received by Christians without, however, dispossessing the Jews.

Even though in Jesus Christ the Covenant was renewed for Christendom, the Jewish people must not be looked upon by Christians as a mere social and historical reality but most of all as a religious one; not as the relic of a venerable and finished past but as a reality alive through the ages. The principal features of this vitality of the Jewish people are its collective faithfulness to the One God; its fervor in studying the Scriptures to discover, in the light of Revelation, the meaning of human life; its search for an identity amidst other men; its constant efforts to re-assemble as a new, unified community. These signs pose questions to us Christians which touch on the heart of our faith: What is the proper mission of the Jews in the divine plan? What expectations animate them, and in what respect are these expectations different from or similar to, our own?

IV. Not to teach anything that does not conform to the spirit of Christ

a) It is most urgent that Christians cease to represent the Jews according to clichés forged by the hostility of centuries. Let us eliminate once and for all and combat under any circumstances, those caricatures unworthy of an honest man and the more so of a Christian. We are thinking, for instance, of that contention tinged with contempt and aversion that the Jew "is not like other people;" or that Jews "are usurious, ambitious, conspiratorial;" or that distortion so frightful because of its consequences, that the Jew is a "deicide." We strongly denounce and condemn these defamatory designations which are still, alas, current among us, openly or in disguise. Anti-Semitism is a heritage from the pagan world but reinforced by pseudo-theological arguments in a Christian climate. Jews merit our attention and esteem, often our admiration — at times also our amicable and brotherly criticism — yet always our love. And it is probably the latter which the Jewish people needed most and in which Christians have been most neglectful.

b) It is a theological, historical, and juridical error to hold the Jewish people without distinction guilty of the Passion and Death of Jesus Christ. The Catechism of the Council of Trent already rejected this error (para I, cap 5,11). If it is true that historically speaking the responsibility for the death of Jesus lies with a number of different Jewish and Roman authorities, the Church holds that Christ in His great love submitted to His passion and death for the sins of all men

61

and for their salvation (*Nostra Aetate*, n. 6). Contrary to what an ancient but contested catechesis has sustained, we must not deduce from the New Testament that the Jewish people were deprived of its election. Scripture as a whole asks us to recognize, on the contrary, that the fidelity of the Jewish people to the Law and Covenant is a sign of the fidelity of God toward His people.

c) It is wrong to oppose Judaism as a religion of fear to Christianity as one of love. The *Shema Yisrael,* the fundamental article of Jewish faith begins: "You shall love the Lord your God," followed by the commandment to love one's neighbor (Lv 19:18). This is also the point of departure for Jesus' preaching, and therefore, a doctrine common to Judaism and Christianity. Feelings for the transcendence and faithfulness of God, His justice and mercy, for repentance and pardon for transgressions are fundamental traits of the Jewish tradition. Christians who appeal to the same values would be wrong in thinking that they no longer have anything to gain from Jewish spirituality.

d) Contrary to established ways of thinking, it must be emphasized that Pharisaic doctrine is not opposed to that of Christianity. The Pharisees sought to make the law come alive in every Jew, by interpreting its commandments in such a way as to adapt them to the various spheres of life. Contemporary research has shown that the Pharisees were no more strangers to the innermost meaning of the law than were the masters of the Talmud. It was not that which Jesus meant when He denounced the attitude of some of them or the formalism of their teaching. On the contrary, it seems that because the Pharisees and first Christians were in certain respects quite close to one another that at times they fought fiercely about the traditions received from the ancients and the interpretation of the Mosaic Law.

V. To gain a fair understanding of Judaism

Christians, if only for their own good, should acquire a true and sincere understanding of Jewish tradition.

a) A genuinely Christian catechesis must stress the topical importance of the entire Bible. The First Covenant was not made invalid by the Second. The former is the root and source, the foundation and the promise. If it is true that the Old Testament renders its ultimate meaning to us only in the light of the New, it is nevertheless required that we should first receive and understand it by itself (2 Tim 3:16). We must not forget that Jesus, by His obedience to the Torah and its prayers, accomplished His ministry within the pale of the Covenant people.

b) We should describe the particular vocation of this people by the "Sanctification of the Name." It is one of the essential dimensions of the synagogue prayer by which the Jewish people, invested with a priestly mission (Ex 19:6), offers all human activity to God and thereby glorifies Him. This vocation makes the life and prayer of the Jewish people a benediction for all the nations of the earth.

c) We would underestimate the precepts of Judaism, were we to consider them mere restrictive practices. Its rites are gestures which interrupt the commonplace existence, reminding those who fulfill them of the sovereignty of God. Devout Jews consider the Sabbath as well as other observances as gifts given by God. Beyond their literal meaning, these ritual acts shed light and joy on the path of the Jew's life (Ps 119). They are a way to "prepare the time," and render thanks for the entire creation. We must, indeed, relate our whole existence to God, as St. Paul urged his brothers (1 Cor 10:30-31).

d) The dispersion of the Jewish people should be understood in the light of its history. Though Jewish tradition considers the trials and exile of the people as a punishment for infidelities (Jer 13:17; 20:21-23), it is nonetheless true that, since the time when Jeremiah addressed his letter to the exiles in Babylon (29:1-23), the life of the Jewish people in the diaspora has also held a positive meaning. Throughout its trials, the Jewish people has been called to "Sanctify the Name," amidst the nations of the world. Christians must constantly combat the anti-Jewish and Manichean temptation to regard the Jewish people as accursed, under the pretext of its constant persecutions. According to the testimony of Scripture (Is 53:2-4), being subjected to persecution is often an effect and reminder of the prophetic vocation.

e) Today more than ever, it is difficult to pronounce a well-considered theological opinion on the return of the Jewish people to "its" land. In this context, we Christians must first of all not forget the gift once made by God to the people of Israel, of a land where it was called to be reunited (cf Gn 12:7; 26:3-4; 28:13; Is 43:5-7; Jer 16:15; Soph 3:20).

Throughout history, Jewish existence has always been divided between life among the nations and the wish for national existence on that land. This aspiration poses numerous problems even to Jews. To understand it, as well as all dimensions of the resulting discussion, Christians must not be carried away by interpretations that would ignore the forms of Jewish communal and religious life, or by political positions that, though generous, are nonetheless hastily arrived at. Christians must take into account the interpretation given by Jews to their ingathering around Jerusalem which, according to their faith, is considered a blessing. Justice is put to the test by this return and its repercussions. On the political level, it has caused confrontations between various claims for justice. Beyond the legitimate divergence of political options, the conscience of the world community cannot refuse the Jewish people, who had to submit to so many vicissitudes in the course of its history, the right and means for a political existence among the nations. At the same time, this right and the opportunities for existence cannot be refused to those who, in the course of local conflicts resulting from this return, are now victims of grave injustice.

Let us, then, turn our eyes toward this land visited by God and let us actively hope that it may become a place where one day all its inhabitants, Jews and non-Jews, can live together in peace. It is an essential question, faced by Christians as well as Jews, whether or not the ingathering of the dispersed Jewish people — which took place under pressure of persecution and by the play of political forces — will despite so many tragic events prove to be one of the final ways of God's justice for the Jewish people and at the same time for all the nations of the earth. How could Christians remain indifferent to what is now being decided in that land?

VI. To promote mutual knowledge and esteem.

Most encounters between Jews and Christians are still marked by mutual ignorance and a certain distrust. Such attitudes have been in the past and could become again in the future, sources of grave misunderstandings and formidable ills. We consider it essential and urgent that the faithful, priests, and all those responsible for education endeavor to create among Christians a better understanding of Judaism, its traditions, customs, and history.

The first condition is that Christians always be respectful of Jews, no matter how they express their Jewishness; that they seek to understand the latter as they understand themselves, instead of judging them by Christian ways of thinking. Christians must respect Jewish convictions, aspirations, and rites, as well as the attachment that Jews bear them. Christians must admit that there are different ways of being a Jew, of considering oneself Jewish, without detriment to the fundamental unity of Jewish existence.

The second condition is that in encounters between Christians and Jews there should be recognized the mutual right to bear witness to one's faith, without being suspected of a disloyal attempt to detach the other from his community and draw him to one's own. Such an intention must be excluded not only out of respect which must apply to dialogue with any person, but for a particular reason to which Christians, and expecially the clergy, must pay more attention. That reason is that the Jews as people have been the object of an "eternal Covenant" without which the "new Covenant" would not even exist.

Far from envisaging the disappearance of the Jewish community, the Church is in search of a living bond with it. Pastors must face these problems with intellectual openness, distrust for their own prejudice, and an acute sense for the psychological conditioning of others. Even if in the present context of a "civilization without frontiers," there occur personal démarches, removed from the determination of the two communities, their mutual esteem must remain unchanged.

VII The Church and the Jewish people

a) The Jewish people is aware of having received, by its particular calling, a universal mission towards the nations. The Church, on the other hand, knows that her own mission is a part of that same universal plan of salvation.

b) Israel and the Church are not complementary institutions; their permanent vis à vis is a sign that the divine plan is not yet complete. Christians and Jews are thus in a situation of mutual contest or, according to St. Paul, of "jealousy" with regard to unity (Rom 11:14; cf Dt 32:21).

c) The words of Jesus Himself and the teaching of Paul testify to the role of the Jewish people in the fulfillment of the ultimate unity of mankind, as a unity of Israel and the nations. Jewish search for unity in our day cannot be removed from the divine plan, nor can it be unrelated to the efforts of Christians for such unity, even though each is proceeding along a different road.

Though Jews and Christians accomplish their vocation along dissimilar lines, history shows that their paths cross incessantly. Is not the Messianic time their common concern? It is desirable that they enter the road of mutual acceptance and appreciation and, repudiating their former enmity, turn toward the Father, with one and the same movement of hope, which will be a promise for the entire world.

Statement by the Synod of Basle, Switzerland. Novemer 1974. Translated from the German.

Concern for the unity of Christ's Church compels us to consider our common heritage with the Jewish people. Together with them, we acknowledge the revelation of the Old Testament. Jesus Christ and the apostles were Jews. The faith of our Jewish brothers, therefore, deserves our particular respect. We share with them the hope for the fulfillment of redemption.

Reviewing the past, we must confirm with regret that an often faulty and hard-hearted presentation of Judaism led to a wrong attitude of Christians towards Jews.

Hence, great care must be taken in religious instruction, liturgical services, adult education, and theological training, to offer a correct interpretation of Jewish self-understanding. The exposition of conflicts, as they present themselves in the New Testament, must conform to recent developments of our insight.

The Synod asks all Christians, in particular those in charge of parishes and dioceses, to spread information on the Jews of our time by means of dialogue and common activities as well as by supporting the work of Christian-Jewish study groups.

A Change of Attitude toward the Jewish People's History of Faith. Catholic Bishops of the Federal Republic of Germany. (Reprinted with kind permission, "Freiburger Rundbrief" XXVII/1975. Translated from the German original.)

Our country's recent political history is darkened by the systematic attempt to wipe out the Jewish people. Apart from some admirable efforts by individuals and groups, most of us during the time of National Socialism formed a church community preoccupied with the threat to our own institutions. We turned our backs to this persecuted Jewish people and were silent about the crimes perpetrated on Jews and Judaism. Many became guilty from sheer fear for their lives. We feel particularly distressed about the fact that Christians even took active part in these persecutions. The honesty of our intention to renew ourselves depends on the admission of this guilt, incurred by our country and our church. Our German church, in particular, must be alert to all tendencies that might diminish human rights and misuse political power. We must assist all those who are now persecuted for racist or other ideological reasons. On our church falls the special obligation of improving the tainted relationship between the Church as a whole and the Jewish people and its religion.

We Germans, in particular, must not deny or over-simplify the redemptive link between the people of the Old Covenant and that of the New, as interpreted and acknowledged by the Apostle Paul. For it was in that sense, too, that we became debtors of the Jewish people. Our speaking of the "God of hope" in the presence of the hopeless horrors of Auschwitz, gains credibility only by the fact that innumerable persons, Jews and Christians, spoke of and called upon this God, even while living in that hell and after escaping from it. This is the task of our people, in view of the attitude of other nations and world public opinion vis à vis the Jewish people. We deem it the particular duty of the German church within the Church as a whole, to work toward a new relationship between Christians on the one hand, and Jews and their history of faith on the other.

d) LATIN AMERICAN STATEMENTS (JOINT JEWISH-CHRISTIAN)

The following joint Resolutions and Recommendations by Jews and Christians mirror the situation in Latin America. Despite urgent requests, we were unable to secure protocols of meetings that took place in Lima and Buenos Aires.

Conclusions and Recommendations of a Meeting between Jews and Christians, in Bogota, Colombia, 1968, organized by CELAM and Anti-Defamation League of B'nai B'rith. Practically all Latin American countries were represented, by rabbis and lay people of the three main currents of Judaism, and Christian bishops, priests, religious, and laity.

1. Community Service

The meeting recommends collaboration free of all prejudice through the medium of existing civic organizations. It recommends contact and common action by Jewish and Christian families, with a view to offering services of a family and social character. The meeting further recommends better realization of the need for joint work. The largest or most representative Jewish and Christian organizations should make contact in each locality, to form joint commissions or name delegates, in order to discover the communities' needs. Possible solutions should be examined, including those involving the mobilization of civic organizations, welfare institutions, and individuals. All joint work should be as widespread as possible, so as to witness to the unity of the two religious communities in furthering human needs.

2. Study and Cultural Exchange

The meeting recommends the establishment and integration of groups of theological experts, for private work and eventual publication of results. Topics for study are, among others: The significance of Israel in Jewish theology; secularization; atheism; salvation in Christianity and Judaism.

CELAM (Episcopal Committee of Latin America) and the corresponding Jewish organizations should encourage the reciprocal establishment of study courses and seminaries in theological departments. Lecture tours by Catholic and Jewish experts should be promoted. Study of the Bible by joint family and student groups is recommended and texts and commentaries of mutual interest to be made available. An address list of persons in Jewish-Christian relations work is to be prepared.

3. Fight Against Prejudice

The meeting proposes to concern itself with discovery of existing mutual prejudice, in schools, seminaries, and families. Text books, catechisms, and prayerbooks, as well as dictionaries and encyclopedias are to be revised, with a view of eliminating every form of mutual prejudice.

The Ecumenical Department of *CELAM* was asked to enlist the cooperation of the Faith Department, to inform all Latin American episcopal conferences of the results of the meeting, and to promote joint meetings for the study of specific problems in Judaeo-Christian dialogue.

4. Shared Worship
The meeting recommends that knowledge of each other's liturgies be promoted and the use of terms in the vocabulary of worship defined.

*Resolutions of the Third Jewish-Catholic Encounter,
organized by the Jewish Congress of Latin America
and the Ecumenical Section of the Episcopal Committee
of Latin America (CELAM)
Sao Paolo, Brazil, April 20-22, 1975.*

Confirming a previous plan (Lima, Peru, 1972), it was decided to arrange regular meetings in the future.

Serious consideration was given to arranging such meetings on a regional and national basis. Where not yet in existence, appropriate organizations should be founded.

It is desirable that educators, group leaders, etc. be trained for the dialogue between Christians and Jews.

CELAM was asked to approach the various national bishops' conferences, for the creation and promotion of commissions or secretariats, according to the orientations and suggestions of the "Commission for Religious Relations with Jews" in Rome. At the same time, the Jewish Congress of Latin America was asked to contact the representative organs of Jewish communities in Latin America, to approach the corresponding commissions of *CELAM*.

It was noted with satisfaction that the first issue of an information sheet on Jewish-Catholic relations, issued jointly by the two above-mentioned organizations, will soon be published.

It was unanimously decided to ask the "Commission for Religious Relations with Jews" to choose a Latin American city for their next meeting place.

II. PROTESTANT DOCUMENTS

a) STATEMENTS BY THE WORLD COUNCIL OF CHURCHES

First Assembly of the WCC, Amsterdam, Holland, 1948
The Christian Approach to the Jews

The Report was received by the Assembly and commended to the churches for their serious consideration and appropriate action.

Introduction
  A concern for the Christian approach to the Jewish people confronts us inescapably, as we meet together to look with open and penitent eyes on man's disorder and to rediscover together God's eternal purpose for His Church. This concern is ours because it is first a concern of God made known to us in Christ. No people in His one world have suffered more bitterly from the disorder of man than the Jewish people. We cannot forget that we meet in a land from which 110,000 Jews were taken to be murdered. Nor can we forget that we meet only five years after the extermination of 6 million Jews. To the Jews our God has bound us in a special solidarity linking our destinies together in His design. We call upon all our churches to make this concern their own as we share with them the results of our too brief wrestling with it.

1. The Church's commission to preach the Gospel to all men
  All of our churches stand under the commission of our common Lord, "Go ye into all the world and preach the Gospel to every creature." The fulfilment of this commission requires that we include the Jewish people in our evangelistic task.

2. The special meaning of the Jewish people for Christian faith
  In the design of God, Israel has a unique position. It was Israel with whom God made His covenant by the call of Abraham. It was Israel to whom God revealed His name and gave His law. It was to Israel that He sent His Prophets with their message of judgment and of grace. It was Israel to whom He promised the coming of His Messiah. By the history of Israel God prepared the manger in which in the fulness of time He put the Redeemer of all mankind, Jesus Christ. The Church has received this spiritual heritage from Israel and is therefore in honour bound to render it back in the light of the Cross. We have, therefore, in humble conviction to proclaim to the Jews, "The Messiah for Whom you wait has come." The promise has been fulfilled by the coming of Jesus Christ.

For many the continued existence of a Jewish people which does not acknowledge Christ is a divine mystery which finds its only sufficient explanation in the purpose of God's unchanging faithfulness and mercy (Rom 11:25-29).

3. Barriers to be overcome

Before our churches can hope to fulfil the commission laid upon us by our Lord there are high barriers to be overcome. We speak here particularly of the barriers which we have too often helped to build and which we alone can remove.

We must acknowledge in all humility that too often we have failed to manifest Christian love towards our Jewish neighbors, or even a resolute will for common social justice. We have failed to fight with all our strength the age-old disorder of man which anti-Semitism represents. The churches in the past have helped to foster an image of the Jews as the sole enemies of Christ, which has contributed to anti-Semitism in the secular world. In many lands virulent anti-Semitism still threatens and in other lands the Jews are subjected to many indignities.

We call upon all the churches we represent to denounce anti-Semitism, no matter what its origin, as absolutely irreconcilable with the profession and practice of the Christian faith. Anti-Semitism is sin against God and man.

Only as we give convincing evidence to our Jewish neighbors that we seek for them the common rights and dignities which God wills for His children, can we come to such a meeting with them as would make it possible to share with them the best which God has given us in Christ.

4. The Christian witness to the Jewish people

In spite of the universality of our Lord's commission and of the fact that the first mission of the Church was to the Jewish people, our churches have with rare exceptions failed to maintain that mission. This responsibility should not be left largely to independent agencies. The carrying on of this mission by special agencies has often meant the singling out of the Jews for special missionary attention, even in situations where they might well have been included in the normal ministry of the Church. It has also meant in many cases that the converts are forced into segregated spiritual fellowship rather than being included and welcomed in the regular membership of the Church.

Owing to this failure our churches must consider the responsibility for missions to the Jews as a normal part of parish work, especially in those countries where Jews are members of the general community. Where there is no indigenous church or where the indigenous church is insufficient for this task it may be necessary to arrange for a special missionary ministry from abroad.

Because of the unique inheritance of the Jewish people, the churches should make provision for the education of ministers specially fitted for this task. Provision should also be made for Christian literature to interpret the Gospel to Jewish people.

Equally, it should be made clear to church members that the strongest argument in winning others for Christ is the radiance and contagion of victorious living and the outgoing of God's love expressed in personal human contacts. As this is expressed and experienced in a genuine Christian fellowship and community the impact of the Gospel will be felt. For such a fellowship there will be no difference between a converted Jew and other church members, all belonging to the same church and fellowship through Jesus Christ. But the converted Jew calls for particular tenderness and full acceptance just because his coming into the Church carries with it often a deeply wounding break with family and friends.

In reconstruction and relief activities the churches must not lose sight of the plight of Christians of Jewish origin, in view of their special suffering. Such provision must be made for their aid as will help them to know that they are not forgotten in the Christian fellowship.

5. *The emergence of Israel as a state*
The establishment of the state "Israel" adds a political dimension to the Christian approach to the Jews and threatens to complicate anti-Semitism with political fears and enmities.

On the political aspects of the Palestine problem and the complex conflict of "rights" involved we do not undertake to express a judgment. Nevertheless, we appeal to the nations to deal with the problem not as one of expediency—political, strategic or economic—but as a moral and spiritual question that touches a nerve centre of the world's religious life.

Whatever position may be taken towards the establishment of a Jewish state and towards the "rights" and "wrongs" of Jews and Arabs, of Hebrew Christians and Arab Christians involved, the churches are in duty bound to pray and work for an order in Palestine as just as may be in the midst of our human disorder; to provide within their power for the relief of the victims of this warfare without discrimination; and to seek to influence the nations to provide a refuge for "Displaced Persons" far more generously than has yet been done.

Recommendations
We conclude this report with the recommendations which arise out of our first exploratory consideration of this "concern" of the churches.

1. *To the member churches of the World Council we recommend:*
that they seek to recover the universality of our Lord's commission by including the Jewish people in their evangelistic work;
that they encourage their people to seek for brotherly contact with and understanding of their Jewish neighbors, and co-operation in agencies combating misunderstanding and prejudice;

that in mission work among the Jews they scrupulously avoid all unworthy pressures or inducements;
that they give thought to the preparation of ministers well fitted to interpret the Gospel to Jewish people and to the provision of literature which will aid in such a ministry.

2. *To the World Council of Churches we recommend:*
that it should give careful thought as to how it can best stimulate and assist the member churches in the carrying out of this aspect of their mission;
that it give careful consideration to the suggestion made by the International Missionary Council that the World Council of Churches share with it a joint responsibility for the Christian approach to the Jews;
that it be *RESOLVED*
That, in receiving the report of this Committee, the Assembly recognize the need for more detailed study by the World Council of Churches of the many complex problems which exist in the field of relations between Christians and Jews, and in particular of the following:

a) the historical and present factors which have contributed to the growth and persistence of anti-Semitism, and the most effective means of combating this evil;

b) the need and opportunity in this present historical situation for the development of co-operation between Christians and Jews in civic and social affairs;

c) the many and varied problems created by establishment of a State of Israel in Palestine.

The Assembly therefore asks that these and related questions be referred to the Central Committee for further examination.

Third Assembly of the WCC, New Delhi, India. 1961.
Resolution on Anti-Semitism

The Third Assembly recalls the following words which were addressed to the churches by the First Assembly of the World Council of Churches in 1948: "We call upon all the churches we represent to denounce anti-Semitism, no matter what its origin, as absolutely irreconcilable with the profession and practice of the Christian faith. Anti-Semitism is a sin against God and man. Only as we give convincing evidence to our Jewish neighbors that we seek for them the common rights and dignities which God wills for His children, can we come to such a meeting with them as would make it possible to share with them the best which God has given us in Christ."
The Assembly renews this plea in view of the fact that situations

continue to exist in which Jews are subject to discrimination and even persecution. The Assembly urges its member churches to do all in their power to resist every form of anti-Semitism. In Christian teaching, the historic events which led to the Crucifixion should not be so presented as to impose upon the Jewish people of today responsibilities which must fall on all humanity, not on one race or community. Jews were the first to accept Jesus and Jews are not the only ones who do not yet recognize Him.

The Faith and Order Commission of the World Council of Churches accepted the following Report, which grew out of joint studies by Faith and Order and the WCC's Committee on the Church and the Jewish People, during the years 1964-1967. It was recommended for further theological study on a wider geographical scale, in Geneva, Switzerland, 1968.

1. Introduction

There is a growing awareness in many churches today that an encounter with the Jews is essential. On various occasions in the past the World Council of Churches has condemned any form of anti-Semitism. It is, however, necessary to think through the theological implications and the complex questions bound up with the Church's relation to the Jewish people in a more explicit and systematic way. We hope that what follows here may be a contribution to such a study. We cannot pretend to offer more than that. We are aware of the shortcomings of this statement, and particularly that differences of opinion among us, which we have not yet been able to resolve, impose limits on what we can say. However, what we offer is, notwithstanding its limitations, new in the history of the World Council. We hope that this statement will stimulate a continuing discussion and will pave the way for a deeper common understanding and eventually a common declaration.

Both in biblical and contemporary language the words "Israel" and "Jews" can have various meanings. To avoid misunderstanding, in this document we have used the term "Israel" only when referring to the people in Old and New Testament times; no present-day political reference is intended or implied. When we speak about the people in post-biblical times we prefer to use the terms "Jews" or "Jewish people", the latter being a collective term designating the Jews all over the world. We find it hard to define in precise terms what it is that makes a Jew a Jew, though we recognize that both ethnic elements and religious traditions play a role.

In drawing up this document we set out to answer two distinct questions which were put to us: 1) in what way does the continuing existence of the Jews have theological significance for the Church, and 2) in what way should Christians give witness of their faith to Jews. The structure of this paper is to a great extent conditioned by this starting-point. It should also be kept in mind that we speak as Christian theologians; we are conscious of the fact that theological statements often have political, sociological or economic implications, even if that is not intended. That consideration, however, cannot be a reason for silence; we merely ask that this paper may be judged on its theological merits.

In our discussions we constantly kept the biblical writings in mind and tried to understand our questions in the light of the Scriptures. We realized that the evidence of the Bible, both Old and New Testaments, is varied and complex, and that we are all in constant danger of arbitrarily excluding parts of it. In re-thinking the place of the Jews in the history of salvation, we should recognize that the question of Israel is very important in parts of the gospels and the Pauline letters, but it seems to be less in evidence in other parts of the New Testament literature, though it is perhaps rarely entirely absent. The problems of interpreting the biblical evidence in regard to this question are just as difficult as they are in regard to other significant theological issues. Being aware of the danger of building one's thinking upon particular proof-texts, we have refrained from pointing to specific verses. We have tried, however, to be faithful to the overall meaning of the Bible and trust that the scriptural basis of what we say will be evident.

II Historical Considerations

The first community of Christians were Jews who had accepted Jesus as the Christ. They continued to belong to the Jewish communities and the relationship between them and their fellow-Jews was close, notwithstanding the tension that existed between them — a tension caused by the fact that the Christian Jews believed that the fulness of time had come in Christ and in the outpouring of the Spirit and that they therefore came to know themselves to be found in one fellowship with Gentiles who also believed in God through Jesus Christ. The two groups of Jews broke apart as the consequence of various facts: for example, the attitude of Christians towards the Law, the persecution of the Stephen group by Jews, the withdrawal from Jerusalem of the Christians during the great uprising 66-73 A.D., the increasing hostility between Jews and Christians which found expression in their respective liturgies, and in other ways. In the same period Christians of Gentile origin came greatly to outnumber the Jewish Christians. From this time on the history of Jews and Christians is one of ever increasing mutual estrangement. After Christianity became the accepted religion of the Roman state, the Jews were discriminated against and often even persecuted by the "Christian" state, more often than not with ecclesiastical support. As a consequence, the so-called "dialogues" between Christian and Jewish theologians which were organized from time to time were never held on a footing of equality; the Jewish partners were not taken seriously.

In the past the existence of Jews outside the Church and their refusal to accept the Christian faith prompted little serious theological questioning in official church circles. Christians generally thought about these questions in very stereotyped ways: the Jews as the Israel of the Old Testament had formerly been God's elect people, but this election had been transferred to the Church after Christ; the continuing existence of the Jews was primarily thought of in terms of divine rejection and retribution, because they were regarded as those who had killed Christ and whose hearts were so hardened that they continued to reject him.

Despite all this the separation between the Church and the Jewish people has never been absolute. In the liturgy of the Church many Jewish elements have been preserved. And when in the middle of the second century Marcion tried to cut all ties by rejecting the Old Testament as God's revelation and by clearing the New Testament as far as possible of all its Old Testament concepts and references, the Church by holding fast to the Old Testament, testified to the continuity between the old and the new covenants. She thereby in fact testified also to the common root and origin of the Church and the Jewish people, although this was not clearly realized; and only few Christians have been aware that this common root meant some kind of special relationship.

At the scholarly and theological level also there has always been contact between the two groups. In the Middle Ages especially, Christian theology and exegesis were strongly influenced by Jews, who for instance transmitted Aristotelian philosophy to them; the influence of Jewish mysticism upon Christian mystics, moreover, has been much stronger than is generally known. In the 16th century among Christians of the Western world a new awareness of their relationship with Jews arose, partly under the influence of humanism with its emphasis on the original biblical languages, partly because of the Reformation. Protestant attitudes were however, by no means always positive. In Pietism a strong love and hope for the Jewish people awoke, which in the 18th and 19th century found expression in the many attempts to come into missionary contact with Jews. But even so, there was little change in the thinking by Christians generally about the Jews. The time of the Enlightenment, with its common move towards toleration, brought improvement in the position of the Jews, at least in Western Europe. This happened in a cultural atmosphere in which there was a tendency to deny the particularity of the Jewish people. Outright anti-Semitism, with its excesses and pogroms, seemed a thing of the past, although in most countries religious and social discrimination remained, the more insidious because it was often not fully conscious.

It is only since the beginning of this century, and even more especially since the last war, that churches, and not merely various individual Christians, have begun to rethink more systematically the nature of their relationship to the Jews. The main theological reason for this is probably the greater emphasis on biblical theology and the increased interest which the Old Testament in particular has received. It is self-evident that this emphasis was to a great extent caused by the preceding outbreak of anti-Semitism in Germany and its rationalization on so-called Christian, ideological grounds. In the realm of biblical scholarship there is today increasing co-operation among Christians and Jews; many Christian theologians are aware of what they have learned from men like Rosenzweig, Buber and other Jewish scholars. The question of what is meant by election and the irrevocability of God's love is being asked again in a new way. The biblically important concept of "covenant" has become more central, and the relationship between the "old" and the "new" covenant is being restudied. In addition, Paul's wrestling with the baffling question of the disobedience of the greater part of his fellow-Jews has come up for consideration.

Besides these theological grounds, two historical events in the last thirty years have caused churches to direct their thinking more than before to their relationship to the Jewish people. In Europe persecution has taken place, greater and more brutal than could have been thought possible in our time, in which some six million Jews were annihilated in the most terrible way, not because of their personal actions or beliefs, but because of the mere fact that they had Jewish grandparents. The churches came to ask themselves whether this was simply the consequence of natural human wickedness, or whether it had also another, theological, dimension.

The second event was the creation of the State of Israel. This is of tremendous importance for the great majority of Jews; it has meant for them a new feeling of self-assurance and security. But this same event has also brought suffering and injustice to Arab people. We find it impossible to give a unanimous evaluation of its formation and of all the events connected with it, and therefore in this study do not make further mention of it. We realize, however, especially in view of the changed situation in the Middle East as a result of the war of June 1967, that also the question of the present State of Israel, and of its theological significance, if any, has to be taken up.

III Theological Considerations

We believe that God formed the people of Israel. There are certainly many factors of common history, ethnic background and religion, which can explain its coming into existence, but according to Old Testament faith as a whole, it was God's own will and decision which made this one distinct people with its special place in history. God is the God of the whole earth and of all nations, but he chose this particular people to be the bearer of a particular promise and to act as his covenant-partner and special instrument. He made himself known specifically to Israel, and showed this people what his will is for men on earth. Bound to him in love and obedience, it was called to live as God wants his people to live. In this way it was to become, as it were, a living revelation to others, in order that they also might come to know, trust, love and obey God. In dealing with Israel, God had in view the other nations; this was the road by which he came to them. In other words, in his love for Israel his love for mankind was manifested; in its election Israel, without losing its own particularity, represented the others.

In the Old Testament Israel is shown to be an imperfect instrument; again and again it was untrue to its calling so that it often obscured rather than manifested God's will on earth. But even in its disobedience it was a witness to God — a witness to his judgment, which however terrible was seen as a form of his grace, for in punishment God was seeking to purify his people and to bring them back to himself; a witness also to his faithfulness and love, which did not let his people go, even when they turned away from him.

We believe that in Jesus Christ God's revelation in the Old Testament finds its fulfilment. Through him we see into the very heart of God, in him we see what it really means to say that God is the God of the covenant and loves man to the very end. As he became the man who was the perfect instrument of God's purpose, he took upon himself the vocation of his people. He, as its representative fulfils Israel's task of obedience. In his resurrection it has become manifest that God's love is stronger than human sin. In him God has forgiven and wiped out sin and in him he created his true covenant-partner.

A part of Israel recognized in Jesus as the Christ the full revelation of God. They believed that in him God himself was present, and that in his death and resurrection God acted decisively for the salvation of the world. Numerically they were perhaps only a very small minority, yet in these "few" God's purpose for the whole of Israel is manifest and confirmed. And together with Israel the Gentiles too were now called to the love and service of God. It cannot be otherwise; for if in Jesus Christ the fulness of time has really come, then the nations also must participate in God's salvation, and the separation of Israel is abolished. This is what the Church is: Israel having come to recognize God in Christ, together with the Gentiles who are engrafted into Israel, so that now Jew and Gentile become one in Christ. It is only in this way that the Church is the continuation of the Israel of the Old Testament, God's chosen people, called upon to testify to his mighty acts for men, and to be his fellow-workers in this world.

Christ himself is the ground and substance of this continuity. This is underlined by the preservation of the Old Testament in the Church as an integral part of her worship and tradition. The existence of Christians of Jewish descent provides a visible manifestation of that same continuity, though many Christians are hardly aware of this. The presence of such members in a Church which in the course of time has become composed predominantly of Gentiles, witnesses to the trustworthiness of God's promises, and should serve to remind the Church of her origin in Israel. We are not advocating separate congregations for them. History has shown the twofold danger which lies in this: the danger of discriminating despite all intention to the contrary, and the danger that such separate congregations tend to evolve sectarian traits. But more important than these considerations is that in Christ the dividing wall has been broken down and Jew and Gentile are to form one new man; thus any separation in the Church has been made impossible.

However, without detracting in any way from what has just been said, we should remember that there is room for all kinds of people and cultures in the Church. This implies that Jews who become Christians are not simply required to abandon their Jewish traditions and ways of thinking; in certain circumstances it may therefore be right to form special groups which are composed mainly of Jewish Christians.

The fact that by far the greater part of Israel did not recognize God in Jesus Christ posed a burning question for Paul, not primarily because of the crucifixion, but because even after Christ's resurrection they still rejected him. The existence of Jews today who do not accept him puts the same question to us, because in this respect the situation today is basically the same as it was in Paul's time.

We are convinced that the Jewish people still have a significance of their own for the Church. It is not merely that by God's grace they have preserved in their faith truths and insights into his revelation which we have tended to forget; some of these are indicated in chapter V. But also it seems to us that by their very existence in spite of all attempts to destroy them, they make it manifest that God has not abandoned them. In this way they are a living and visible sign of God's faithfulness to men, an indication that he also upholds those who do not find it possible to recognize him in his Son. While we see their continuing existence as pointing to God's love and mercy, we explicitly reject any thought of considering their sufferings during the ages as a proof of any special guilt. Why, in God's purpose, they have suffered in that way, we as outsiders do not know. What we do know, however, is the guilt of Christians who have all too often stood on the side of the persecutors instead of the persecuted.

Conscious of this guilt we find it impossible to speak in a generalizing way of Christian obedience over against Jewish disobedience. It is true that we believe that Jesus Christ is the truth and the way for every man, and that for everyone faith in him is salvation. But we also know that it is only by grace that we have come to accept him and that even in our acceptance we are still in many ways disobedient. We have therefore no reason to pride ourselves over against others. For Christians as well as Jews can live only by the forgiveness of sin, and by God's mercy.

We believe that in the future also God in his faithfulness will not abandon the Jewish people, but that his promise and calling will ultimately prevail so as to bring them to their salvation. This is to us an assurance that we are allowed to hope for the salvation of all who do not yet recognize Christ. So long as the Jews do not worship with the Church the one God and Father of Jesus Christ, they are to us a perpetual reminder that God's purpose and promise are not yet realized in their fulness, that we have still much to hope for the world, looking for the time when the Kingdom of God will become plainly and gloriously manifest.

All this we can say together. However, this considerable agreement, for which we are grateful indeed, should not conceal the fact that when the question is raised of the theological identity of Israel with the Jewish people of today we find ourselves divided. This division is due not only to the differences in the interpretation of the biblical evidence, but also in the weight which is given to various passages. We might characterize our differences, rather schematically, as follows:

Some are convinced that, despite the elements of continuity that admittedly exist between present day Jews and Israel, to speak of the continued election of the Jewish people alongside the Church is inadmissible. It is the Church alone, they say, that is theologically speaking, the continuation of Israel as the people of God, to which now all nations belong. Election and vocation are solely in Christ, and are to be grasped in faith. To speak otherwise is to deny that the one people of God, the Church, is the body of Christ which cannot be broken. In Christ it is made manifest that God's love and his promises apply to all men. The Christian hope for the Jews is the same as it is for all men: that they may come to the knowledge of the truth, Jesus Christ our Lord. This does not imply any denial of the distinctive and significant witness to Christ which the Jews still bear. For their continued separate existence is the direct result of the dual role which Israel as God's elect people has played: through them salvation has come to the world, and they represented at the crucial time of human history man's rejection of God's salvation offered in Christ.

Others of us are of the opinion that it is not enough merely to assert some kind of continuity between the present-day Jews—whether religious or not—and ancient Israel, but that they actually are still Israel, i.e. that they still are God's elect people. These would stress that after Christ the one people of God is broken asunder, one part being the Church which accepts Christ, the other part Israel outside the Church, which rejects him, but which even in this rejection remains in a special sense beloved by God. They see this election manifested specifically in the fact that the existence of the Jewish people in this world still reveals the truth that God's promises are irrevocable, that he will uphold the covenant of love which he has made with Israel. Further they see this continuing election in the fact that God has linked the final hope of the world to the salvation of the Jews, in the day when he will heal the broken body of his one people, Israel and the Church.

These two views, described above, should however not be understood as posing a clear-cut alternative. Many hold positions somewhere in between, and without glossing over the real disagreements which exist, in some cases these positions can be so close, that they seem to rest more on different emphases than to constitute real contradictions. But even where our positions seem practically irreconcilable, we cannot be content to let the matter rest as it is. For the conversation among us has only just begun and we realize that in this question the entire self-understanding of the Church is at stake.

IV. The Church and Her Witness

In the foregoing it is set forth that the Church stands in a unique relationship to the Jews. Every one who accepts Christ and becomes a member of his Church shares thereby in this special relation, being brought face to face with the Jewish people. That is to say that the problem we are dealing with in this paper is not one which confronts only the so-called Western churches, but concerns every Christian of whatever race, cultural or religious background he may be. So too the Old Testament is not only of importance for those whose culture is to a greater or lesser degree rooted in it, but becomes also the spiritual heritage of those Christians whose own ethnic culture is not touched by it.

The existence of this unique relationship raises the question as to whether it conditions the way in which Christians have to bear witness of Jesus to Jews.

We all agree that the Church is the special instrument of God, which is called to testify in her word and her life to his love revealed in its fulness in his Son. She has to proclaim that in Christ's cross and resurrection it has become manifest that God's love and mercy embrace all men. Moreover, being rooted in his reconciliation, she is called to cross all frontiers of race, culture and nationality, and all other barriers which separate man from man. Therefore we are convinced that no one can be excluded from her message of forgiveness and reconciliation; to do otherwise would be disobedience to the Lord of the Church and a denial of her very nature, a negation of her fundamental openness and catholicity.

In the World Council of Churches much thinking has been done about the question of how the Church can give her witness in such a way that she respects the beliefs and convictions of those who do not share her faith in Christ, and perhaps, with God's help, bring them in full freedom to accept it. It is agreed that in an encounter with non-Christian people real openness is demanded, a willingness to listen to what the other has to say, and a readiness to be questioned by him and learn from his insights. This means that at all times Christians have to guard against an arrogant or paternalistic attitude. Moreover, the way in which they approach different men in different circumstances cannot be a single one; they should do their utmost to gain a real understanding of the life and thinking of the non-Christian, for only thereby can they speak to his situation in their witness.

The very fact that the particular situation in which the Christian witness is given must always be taken into account, applies of course also to the Jews. Moreover, where they are concerned this consideration receives a special dimension, for with no other people does the Church have such close ties. Christians and Jews are rooted in the same divine history of salvation, as has already been shown; both claim to be heirs of the same Old Testament. Christian and Jewish faiths share also a common hope that the world and its history are being led by God to the full realization and manifestation of his Kingdom.

However, in an encounter between Christians and Jews not only the common ties are to be considered but also their agelong alienation and the terrible guilt of discrimination which Christians share with the world, and which in our own time has culminated in the gas-chamber and the destruction of a large part of European Jewry. Though certainly not all Christians are equally guilty and though anti-Semitism has played no particular role in the Oriental and in the so-called younger churches, we all have to realize that Christian words have now become disqualified and suspect in the ears of most Jews. Therefore often the best, and sometimes perhaps even the only way in which Christians today can testify to the Jewish people about their faith in Christ may be not so much in explicit words but rather by service.

We all are thus basically of one mind about the actual form which in practice the Christian encounter with the Jewish people has to take. We differ, however, among ourselves when we try to analyse and to formulate this common attitude in theological terms. Our differences are bound up with differences in ecclesiology, or rather with the different ecclesiological points on which we lay stress. If the main emphasis is put on the concept of the Church as the body of Christ, the Jewish people are seen as being outside. The Christian attitude to them is considered to be in principle the same as to men of other faiths and the mission of the Church is to bring them, either individually or corporately, to the acceptance of Christ, so that they become members of his body. Those who hold this view would generally want to stress that besides service to the Jews it is also legitimate and even necessary to witness in a more explicit way as well, be it through individuals, or special societies, or churches.

If, on the other hand, the Church is primarily seen as the people of God, it is possible to regard the Church and the Jewish people together as forming the one people of God, separated from one another for the time being, yet with the promise that they will ultimately become one. Those who follow this line of thinking would say that the Church should consider her attitude towards the Jews theologically and in principle as being different from the attitude she has to all other men who do not believe in Christ. It should be thought of more in terms of ecumenical engagement in order to heal the breach than of missionary witness in which she hopes for conversion.

Again it should be pointed out that these views are not static positions; there are gradual transitions between the two and often it is more a question of a more-or-less than of an either-or. That is in the nature of the matter. For the Church must be thought of both as the body of Christ and as the people of God, and these two concepts express the one reality from different angles.

But even though we have not yet reached a common theological evaluation of the Christian encounter with Jews, we all emphatically reject any form of "proselytizing", in the derogatory sense which the word has come to carry in our time, where it is used for the corruption of witness in cajolery, undue pressure or intimidation, or other improper methods.

V. *Ecumenical Relevance*

We are convinced that the Church's re-thinking of her theology with regard to the question of Israel and her conversation with the Jewish people can be of real importance to the ecumenical movement. In this way questions are posed which touch the foundation and the heart of Christian faith. Though these questions are also being asked for other reasons, it is our experience that here they are being put in a particularly penetrating form. Because there is no doctrine of Christian theology which is not touched and influenced in some way by this confrontation with the Jewish people, it is impossible for us here to develop fully its implications. We can only indicate some salient points.

1. The documents of the Old Testament belong to the heritage which the churches have received from and have in common with the Jews. In a theological encounter of the two groups the question of the right understanding of these writings will necessarily come to the fore, the Jews placing them in the context of the Talmud and Midrash, the churches in that of the New Testament. Thereby Christians are called upon to analyze the criteria they use in their interpretation of the Bible. Clarity in this respect will help the churches in their search together for the biblical truth.

2. The Old Testament is also part of the common heritage that lies beyond the separation of the churches themselves. Differences in its evaluation and interpretation may result in different understandings of the New Testament. When in their meeting with Jewish theologians the churches are driven to reconsider whether they have understood the Old Testament aright, and perhaps coming to new insights into it, it may well help them also to understand the Gospel in a deeper and fuller way and so overcome one-sided and different conceptions which keep them apart.

3. Jewish faith regards itself as being based on God's revelation written down in the Bible as it is interpreted and actualized in the ongoing tradition of the Jewish believing community. Therefore, in their theological dialogue with Jews the churches will be confronted with the question of tradition and Scripture. When this problem, which has been a cause of dissension between Christians for a long time, is considered in this new setting, the churches may gain insights which can contribute to a greater understanding and agreement among themselves.

4. The emphasis made by Jews in their dialogue with Christians on justice

and righteousness in this world reminds the churches of the divine promise of a new earth and warns them not to express their eschatological hope onesidedly in other-worldy terms.

Equally, reflection in the light of the Bible on the Jewish concept of man as God's covenant-partner working for the sanctification of the world and for the bringing in of the Kingdom should prompt the churches to reconsider their old controversy over the co-operation of man in salvation.

5. The existence of Jews, both those who have become Christians and those who have not, compels the churches to clarify their own belief about election. They must ask themselves whether election is not a constitutive element in God's action with men, whether it does not have an unshakable objectivity which precedes the response of those who are elected, but which on the other hand requires ever anew acceptance by faith, realized in human acts of obedience. A study of these questions may bring closer together those who stress the prevenient grace of God and those who put the main accent on the human decision of faith.

VI. Some Implications

Finally we want to point to some implications of this study. Needless to say, they can be indicated only briefly; we hope that in the future some of these points will be taken up and further elaborated and acted upon. In this connection we recall the following words of the Third Assembly in New Delhi, which renewed the plea against anti-Semitism of the First Assembly in 1948, adding that "the Assembly urges its member churches to do all in their power to resist every form of anti-Semitism. In Christian teaching, the historic events which led to the Crucifixion should not be so presented as to impose upon the Jewish people of today responsibilities which must fall on all humanity, and not on one race or community. Jews were the first to accept Jesus and Jews are not the only ones who do not yet recognize Him."

The last sentences of the statement just quoted refer to the question of the responsibility of the Jews today for the crucifixion. This question has both a historical and a theological dimension. 1) Modern scholarship has generally come to the conclusion that it is historically wrong to hold the Jewish people of Jesus' time responsible as a whole for his death. Only a small minority of those who were in Jerusalem were actively hostile to him, and even these were only indirectly instrumental in bringing about his death: the actual sentence was imposed by the Roman authorities. Moreover, it is impossible to hold the Jews of today responsible for what a few of their forefathers may have participated in nearly twenty centuries ago. 2) Theologically speaking we believe that this small minority, acting together with the Roman authorities, expressed the sin and blindness common to all mankind. Those passages in the New Testament which charge the Jews with the Crucifixion of Jesus must be read within the wider biblical understanding of Israel as representative of all men. In their rejection of Christ our own rejection of him is mirrored.

We recommended that, especially in religious instruction and preaching, great care be taken not to picture the Jews in such a way as to foster inadvertently a kind of "Christian" anti-Semitism. In addition to the way in which the Crucifixion is often taught, we have in mind, among other things, the historically mistaken image often given of the Pharisees, the misconception of the Law of the Old Testament and its so-called legalism, and the stress repeatedly placed upon the disobedience of the Jews according to the Old and New Testaments, without it being made sufficiently clear that those who denounced this disobedience were also Jews, one with their people notwithstanding their denunciation.

Similarly, some Christian prayers contain expressions which, whatever their meaning formerly was, can easily promote misunderstanding today. We feel that it would help if the churches would re-examine both traditional liturgies and also lessons, hymns and other texts used in worship from the point of view set out in this document.

The fact that the Jewish people is of continued significance for the Church should also have its effect on the way history is presented. Because of this special relationship all through the ages, church history cannot rightly be taught without taking into account its impact on the history of the Jews, and vice versa. We are of the opinion that theological teaching and text books are in general inadequate in this respect and need to be reconsidered and supplemented.

There is a general tendency among Christians to equate the faith of the Old Testament with Jewish religion today. This is an oversimplification which does not do justice to Jewish understanding of the Old Testament and to subsequent developments. Here the oral law must be specially mentioned, for it has played such a central role in shaping Jewish life and thought, and still continues to be of paramount importance for large groups.

We should also be aware that many, while affirming that they belong to the Jewish people, do not call themselves believing Jews. For a real encounter with the Jews we consider it imperative to have knowledge and genuine understanding of their thinking and their problems both in the secular and in the religious realm. We should always remain aware that we are dealing with actual, living people in all their variety, and not with an abstract concept of our own.

We have often been aware in our discussions that no problem should be examined in isolation. Nor should this one be, since there may be a danger that, instead of reducing anti-Semitism, we may even increase it by concentrating on this issue.

Through our study together it has been brought home to us that much thinking still has to be done, and how impossible it is to ignore or avoid the theological questions in this area. We feel assured that an ongoing encounter with Jews can mean a real enrichment of our faith. Christians should therefore be alert to every such possibility, both in the field of social co-operation and especially on the deeper level of theological discussion. We realize that at the moment many Jews are not willing to be involved with Christians in a common dialogue; in that case Christians must respect this expressed or silent wish and not force themselves upon them. But when such conversation is possible, it should be held in a spirit of mutual respect and openness, searching together and questioning one another, trusting that we together with the Jews will grow into a deeper understanding of the revelation of the God of Abraham, Isaac and Jacob. What form this further understanding may take, we must be willing to leave in His hands, confident that He will lead both Jews and Christians into the fulness of His truth.

b) STATEMENTS BY VARIOUS CHURCH GROUPS

*In 1964, the Department of World Mission of the Lutheran
World Federation, to which about 75 million Lutherans in
various parts of the world belong, called together theologians,
pastors and mission specialists for a Consultation
On The Church And The Jewish People, in Logumkloster, Denmark.
The participants adopted a series of statements representing
a broad consensus.*

1. The Church and Israel

Those who share in the Christian inheritance "must recognize a grateful responsibility for the original heirs. It follows, therefore, that the Church will pray for the Jews daily, especially in its Sunday worship".

2. Mission and Dialogue

This statement declares that "the witness to the Jewish people is inherent in the content of the Gospel, and from the commission received from Christ, the Head of the Church," and recommends that it be "pursued in the normal activity of the Christian Congregation, which reflects itself in the Christian witness of the individual members. It is a Christian responsibility to seek respectfully to understand both the Jewish people and their faith. Therefore, responsible conversations between Christians and Jews are to be desired and welcomed. Such conversations presuppose the existence of common ground on which Christians and Jews may meet, as well as points of difference . . . The conversations do not assume an equating of the religions, nor do they require that Christians abstain from making their witness as a natural outgrowth of the discussions. Similarly Christians will listen gladly as Jews explain their insights of faith."

3. The Church and Anti-Semitism

"Anti-Semitism is an estrangement of man from his fellow-men. As such it stems from human prejudice and is a denial of the dignity and equality of men. But anti-Semitism is primarily a denial of the image of God in the Jew; it represents a demonic form of rebellion against the God of Abraham, Isaac and Jacob; and a rejection of Jesus the Jew, directed upon his people. 'Christian' anti-Semitism is spiritual suicide.

"This phenomenon presents a unique question to the Christian Church, especially in light of the long terrible history of Christian culpability for anti-Semitism. No Christian can exempt himself from involvement in this guilt. As Lutherans, we confess our own peculiar guilt, and we lament with shame the responsibility which our Church and her people bear for this sin. We can only ask God's pardon and that of the Jewish people. There is no ultimate defeat of anti-Semitism short of a return to the living God in the power of his grace and through the forgiveness of Jesus Christ our Lord. At the same time, we must pledge ourselves to work in concert with others at practical measures for overcoming manifestations of this evil within and without the Church and for reconciling Christians with Jews.

"Toward this end, we urge the Lutheran World Federation and its member Churches:

a) To examine their publications for possible anti-Semitic references, and to remove and oppose false generalizations about Jews. Especially reprehensible are the notions that Jews, rather than all mankind, are responsible for the death of Jesus the Christ, and that God has for this reason rejected his covenant people. Such examination and reformation must also be directed to pastoral practice and preaching references. This is our simple duty under the commandment common to Jews and Christians: 'Thou shalt not bear false witness against thy neighbor.'

b) To oppose and work to prevent all national and international manifestations of anti-Semitism, and in all our work acknowledge our great debt of gratitude to those Jewish people who have been instruments of the Holy Spirit in giving us the Old and New Testaments and in bringing into the world Jesus Christ our Lord.

c) To call upon our congregations and people to know and to love their Jewish neighbors as themselves; to fight against discrimination and persecution of Jews in their communities; to develop mutual understanding, and to make common cause with the Jewish people in matters of spiritual and social concern, especially in fostering human rights."

The General Board of the National Council of the
Churches of Christ in the United States of America
adopted the following Resolution on Jewish-Christian
Relations. 1964.

The Resolution states: "We confess that sometimes as Christians we have given way to anti-Semitism. We have even used the events of the Crucifixion to condemn the Jewish people." It urges its constituent communions to seek true dialogue with the religious bodies of the Jewish community.

The House of Bishops of the Episcopal Church
issued a statement on "Deicide and the Jews". St. Louis, Mo., 1964.

The poison of anti-Semitism has causes of a political, national, psychological, social, and economic nature. It has often sought religious justification in the events springing from the crucifixion of Jesus. Anti-Semitism is a direct contradiction of Christian doctrine. Jesus was a Jew, and, since the Christian Church is rooted in Israel, spiritually we are Semites.

The charge of deicide against the Jews is a tragic misunderstanding of the inner significance of the crucifixion. To be sure, Jesus was crucified by *some* soldiers at the instigation of *some* Jews. But, this cannot be construed as imputing corporate guilt to every Jew in Jesus' day, much less the Jewish people in subsequent generations. Simple justice alone proclaims the charge of a corporate or inherited curse on the Jewish people to be false.

Furthermore, in the dimension of faith the Christian understands that all men are guilty of the death of Christ, for all have in some manner denied Him; and since the sins that crucified Christ were common human sins, the Christian knows that he himself is guilty. But he rejoices in the words and spirit of his Lord who said for the Roman soldiers and for all responsible for His crucifixion, "Father, forgive them, for they know not what they do."

This report of the Committee on the Church and the Jews was
presented to the Commission on World Mission of the Lutheran
World Federation at its annual meeting in Asmara, Ethiopia, in 1969.
The report was received by the Commission for transmission
to the member churches of the LWF for their study and consideration.
At this time the statement stands as a document of the
Committee only.

1. We as Christians can only speak of the Jewish people if we say that we all are human beings standing under God's judgment and in need of his forgiveness. We are all men and women before we are Jews or Christians. What we say here in a special way about the Jews must be understood in the light of this assertion.

The relationship between Jews and Christians has been confused through the centuries by two wrong assumptions. The first assumption falsifies the Christian understanding by seeing the Jews of all times as identical with that Jewish group which in the first century rejected Jesus of Nazareth as Messiah. The second falsifies the Jewish understanding by seeing all Christians as in principle involved in the hate and persecution which were inflicted on the Jews by the official church and by nations claiming a Christian tradition. While this Committee claims no competence to remove the existing negative opinions held by Jews, it must contribute to the task of eliminating all those barriers raised by past and present Christian misunderstanding which stand in the way of our conversation with the Jews and our understanding of their faith.

We shall have to engage in an ongoing encounter with Jews and Judaism which takes seriously both Jewish and Christian history. In deepening the Jewish-Christian relationship we expect to find ways of understanding each other which have been lost due to historical circumstances. Theological education—and the teaching of church history in particular—will have to undergo considerable revision if this is to be done. Teachers and pastors must be given information and materials so that in their interpreting of Biblical texts they will be sensitive to the false assumptions Christians have made.

The distinction between law and gospel which in Lutheran tradition becomes a key for interpreting the whole Scriptural revelation is connected with this hermeneutical problem. This specific emphasis places a particular burden on Jewish-Lutheran relations. But for this reason it lends increased urgency to theological encounter. As Lutherans we believe, on the basis of Paul's witness, that it is God's action in Christ which justifies the sinner. Thus we cannot speak about the law and about righteousness as though it were obedience which lays the foundation for relationship to God. The theological issue here touches both Jewish-Christian dialogue and Christian use of the Old Testament. Our understanding can be traced to Luther and his reception through Augustine of certain Pauline motifs. It is possible, however, that our whole outlook has been shaped and our relationship to the Jewish people vitiated by a strongly negative understanding of the law and its function. This, it seems to us, might well be a matter for consideration by the Lutheran World Federation Commission on Theology in co-operation with a possible future Committee on the Church and the Jews.

2.   As we try to grasp the theological meaning of the problem we face, we recognize two aspects of the Christian understanding of God's self-disclosure, both of which lead us to the limits of human perception and speech. The first is the fact that with the coming of Jesus into the world a development began which is incomprehensible in its dimensions. It can only be described as an act of God's love for all men. In the moment when,

according to Christian faith, God acted to bring his revelation to its fulfilment, among those who had first received his revelation many did not find themselves able to respond in faith to what God was now doing in Jesus of Nazareth. In spite of this rejection, however, God's saving grace found a way into the world and no human guilt or rejection could negate it. The faith and the universal proclamation that God became man, that God was in Christ reconciling the world unto himself, that Jesus of Nazareth was the Son of God, is an offence to human wisdom and particularly to the religious view of God's glory. It is as if God had of necessity to meet rejection and to suffer the consequences of his love in order to bring life and salvation to mankind.

The second aspect is closely related to the first. Because Jesus took upon himself his cross and became obedient unto death, God raised him from the dead. His death and resurrection constitute a special Christian hope for the whole world. This implies the crucial paradox that for the Christian faith there is a divine future for mankind since Jesus the Nazarene was rejected. Thus we are here directed toward the mystery of God's inscrutable ways with men.

Mystery and paradox—the point where human logic leads no further—stand at the center of all Christian thought. That is the case with christology, but it is equally true of eschatology, and it applies to ecclesiology as well. God has not only prepared a future for all mankind, but has bound this future to the cross and resurrection of the man Jesus of Nazareth. It is our conviction that the central position of the cross and resurrection of Jesus has fundamental consequences for the understanding of the church. This was perceived and expressed in a unique way by Luther. He did not accept identification of the elect people of God with a specific ecclesiological tradition. This view has led to the fatal alternatives of medieval church-centered theology, in which the Jewish people were treated from a position of superiority. Luther opposed any kind of a "theology of glory", i.e. any attempt to see and proclaim God and his deeds and works (including the church) primarily in terms of might, of lordship, of victory and triumph. The theological paradox which confronted Luther in his historical situation, however, proved to be too much for him. This one can see from his later writings against the Jews. In these polemic tracts a theology of glory does break in. Luther's anxiety about the church's existence became so strong that he found himself no longer able to let the future rest in God's hands but, in anticipation of what he read to be God's future judgment, called upon the secular arm to effect that judgment in the present. In doing so he overstepped the bounds of what lies in human authority to do, to say nothing of love. The consequences of this are still with us. The lessons which the church has had to learn in the midst of the holocausts of our century compel us to find a new, more profound, more sober, and at the same time more Christian attitude.

Because of the deep and tragic involvement of men of Christian

89

tradition in the persecution of the Jewish people, the cruel and dangerous anti-Jewish attacks in some of the writings of the old Luther and the continuing threats in our time to the existence of the Jews as a community, we assert our Christian responsibility for their right to exist as Jews.

3.   Jews, on their side, insist that there can be mutual respect and dialogue only if the "legitimacy" of Judaism is recognized by Christians. We believe that this includes not only ethnic and political but also religious factors. What does it mean for us to acknowledge its "legitimacy"? Remembering past Christian criticism of Judaism, Jews demand of Christians recognition of Judaism as a "living" religion. Can such recognition be given? Does it mean that we see two separate but necessary ministries within the one economy of salvation? Is it possible to acknowledge that the survival of Judaism is an act of God without also saying that this survival is a definitive event of salvation history? Does affirmation of the survival or acknowledgement of the legitimacy of Judaism cancel the responsibility of the Christian to bear witness to the Jew at the right time and in the proper way?

In the light of these questions we offer the following affirmations:

We as Lutherans affirm our solidarity with the Jewish people. This solidarity is legitimized in God's election and calling into being in Abraham's seed a people of promise, of faith, and of obedience peculiar unto him, a people whose unity will one day become manifest when "all Israel" will be saved. The Lutheran churches, therefore, may not appropriate the term "people of God" and "Israel" to the church in such a way as to deny that they applied in the first instance to the Jewish people. They may not assert continuity of the church with the covenant people of Abraham in such a way as to question the fact that present-day Judaism has its own continuity with Old Testament Israel.

This our solidarity with the Jewish people is to be affirmed not only despite the crucifixion of Jesus, but also because of it. Through his death Jesus has brought about reconciliation with God, has broken down the barriers between men, and has established a ministry of reconciliation which encompasses all men, both Jews and Gentiles.

This our solidarity with the Jewish people is grounded in God's unmerited grace, his forgiveness of sin and his justification of the disobedient. Whenever we Christians, therefore, speak about "rejection" and "faith", "disobedience" and "obedience" in such a way that "rejection" and "disobedience" are attributes of Jews while "faith" and "obedience" are attributes of Christians, we are not only guilty of the most despicable spiritual pride, but we foster a pernicious slander, denying the very ground of our own existence: grace, forgiveness, and justification.

After all that has happened, the existence of the Jewish people in the world today cannot therefore be seen in the first instance as a problem to be encountered, much less as an embarrassment to be faced by the churches, but as a profound cause for wonder and hope. Despite all the inhuman actions of men and the frightful ambiguities of history, God remains faithful to his promise. We have here tangible evidence that God's grace is yet at work, countering the demonic powers of destruction and guaranteeing a future for mankind which will bring the full unity of God's people.

In understanding ourselves as people of the new covenant which God has made in Jesus the Christ, we Christians see the Jewish people as a reminder of our origin, as a partner in dialogue to understand our common history, and as a living admonition that we, too, are a pilgrim people, a people *en route* toward a goal that can only be grasped in hope. The church, therefore, may never so understand the Word which has been entrusted to it, the Baptism which it must administer, and the Holy Supper which it has been commanded to celebrate as possessions which give Christians superiority over the Jews. The church can only administer in humility the mysteries which God has committed to it— preaching the crucified and risen Christ, baptizing into his death, showing forth his death till he come.

The word which our churches, in bearing witness to Jesus the Christ, must share with Jews as with other men is a joyful message of imperishable hope. This message shows forth a time when God's purpose with his covenant in Abraham and with his covenant in Jesus the Christ will be fulfilled. Then God overcomes all blindness, faithlessness, and disobedience and will be all in all.

This Statement was adopted by the Synod of the Reformed Church, Holland. 1970. (From an English version.)
Israel: People, Land and State. Suggestions for a theological evaluation.

I. Introduction

Why are we talking about the State of Israel?
1. As Christians we are in a special way concerned with and tied to the biblical people of Israel. The Father of Jesus Christ, in whom we believe, is the God of Israel. Therefore Israel is connected with our faith in God. The church is called upon to proclaim its faith in God and its connection with the people of Israel is part of this proclamation.
2. That Israel of which the Bible of OT and NT speaks has not disappeared. The Jewish people, as it appears in our time, is its

continuation. As a matter of history this cannot well be questioned. That does not mean that the people of today is identical with the people of old; 19 centuries lie between. But a direct historical line runs from the former Israel to the people of today. Therefore we use the names "Jewish people" and "people of Israel" indiscriminately in the following. Similarly, the church of our times is not identical with the church of the apostles, but it certainly is its continuation. That is to say, it is the same church.

3. If as Christians we feel ourselves connected with the biblical Israel, the implication is that there is also a special connection between us and the Jewish people of today. It is an essential part of the task of Christians to ponder upon this. Our Hervormde Kerk was one of the first to express its thoughts on the subject. Today the State of Israel is one of the forms in which the Jewish people appear. We would be talking in a void and closing our eyes to reality, if today we were to think about the Jewish people without taking the State of Israel explicitly into consideration.

4. In this report we are specifically concerned with the question whether the State of Israel has a particular relevance for Christian faith. What follows should be read with this restricted question in mind. It has not been our purpose to give a more or less complete exposition of the election of Israel or the relation between the church and Israel. Nor have we tried to give directions for a political solution. We speak as Christians who believe that reflection on the Jewish people and the State of Israel is a task laid upon us by our faith. Therefore we address ourselves primarily to our own church and to the other churches. We expect them to read this report as a thinking through of the problem from the point of view of faith. We understand that what we say necessarily has political consequences, and we do not want to avoid them. Faith has consequences in the political realm, and that is certainly the case when we speak about the Jewish people. We cannot impose our view on politicians of the West or the East, nor on Israel or the Arabs. Muslims and Jews may even wonder why we meddle in their affairs and may doubt whether what we say helps their cause. But we cannot keep silent about what we have understood on the basis of our Christian faith. More than once we shall come up against questions which we cannot answer. That is not surprising; Israel is put in a special place by God; therefore it is a mystery which can never be fully made transparent.

II. The Jewish People in the Old Testament

Israel is in its historical reality the chosen people.

5. The Israel about which the OT speaks was a fact in the world. It consisted of men of flesh and blood, who dwelt in a certain land and had a visible history with treaties, wars, victories and defeats.

6. However, according to this people's testimony of faith, upon which also, thanks to Christ, our faith as Christians is built, it was a people unlike all other peoples. That fact is exclusively based on God's election. He promised that it would be a people before it existed — and only afterwards did it become a people. He assigned it a land with which it was not connected by nature — and afterwards it came into this land. He made a covenant with it and made known to it his will, and this became the tie which bound it together as a people.

7. Therefore the Jewish people of the OT are as a historical reality, the elected people. Here the elective acts of God, which are based on nothing but his sovereign love, obtained a visible form upon this earth amidst the nations. Here it has become clear that God's election is not a mere idea, but that it enters the world in all concreteness. Therefore this people has to be considered from two points of view: (1) historically it is a people subject to human failure and all the vicissitudes of history. (2) Because it is the people to which God has bound himself in a special way, in the history of Israel we are somehow indirectly dealing with God. It is in it that he reveals himself to faith.

8. God had chosen this people for himself; he had formed it and set it apart. This was known by Israel and testified to in its faith. But there was always the danger that it might separate this act of election from the God who elected. Then it regarded the election as a possession on which it could count; and then it was necessary for the prophets to remind their people that their being chosen was based solely on the free grace of God. Israel should know that it could never lay claim to this grace of God as if it were a right. But Israel was also to know that its God was faithful and dependable. Therefore it could trust him, who had made it his chosen people. That is to say, we cannot set faith in the electing God in opposition to the grateful and wondering recognition of being-elected. Election as the free act of God and being-elected, as the being-determined by this act, belong together; the latter is the converse of the former.

9. In its testimonies of faith Israel understood its election as a gift of grace. In many passages of the OT there is a note of grateful wonder about the great privilege of being the special treasure of God and knowing him and his will (cf Ex 19:5,6). But the prophets in particular continuously reminded their people that this privilege carried with it a special responsibility: Israel should walk according to righteousness; its privilege should be a blessing to the nations. Its election was both gift and task. Israel was not to forget that its God is the God of the whole earth and of all nations, and that in his love God wants to disclose himself to all. In that light the people were to see their election.

The Land

10. In its faith Israel regarded its tie with the land as a unique one. It had no natural right to the land, and was not allowed to deal with it as if the land were its possession to which it could lay claim. It was the land allotted by God to his people, the land which God had already promised to the patriarchs. Even in a time when Israel dwelt already in the land and had possession of it, it remained the "promised land," the gift of grace which

was inseparably bound up with God's love. In other words, Israel was always convinced that the land was an essential element of the covenant.

11. According to the entire OT in all its parts the chosen people and the promised land belong together, owing to God. The land was the place allotted to this people in order that they might realize their vocation as God's people to form a holy society. Again and again the prophets stress the point that the land is promised and given for the sake of this calling. When the people did not. come up to their vocation as a chosen people, the prophets threatened them with expulsion. Exile was understood by them as a sign of divine judgement, and return was understood as God's renewed gracious turning towards his people and as a new possibility, granted by him, for them to live according to their calling. Being allowed to dwell in the land could be regarded as a visible sign of God's election and as a concrete form of salvation.

12. We have said above that for Israel its election was no goal in itself, but was directed towards the future: through the fulfillment of the destiny of the people of God and through what God does to this people, the nations also shall get to know God and shall turn to him. The dwelling of Israel in the land also partook of this directedness towards the future. This perspective in which the promised land is put comes clearly to the fore in the preaching of the prophets in the time of the exile. When they speak about the return to the land, they have in mind the historical situation; however, they speak in terms which go far beyond the historical, actual moment. It was the firm conviction of the people of the OT that they could reach their real destiny as God's covenant-people only in the land of Palestine and that the realization of this destiny was closely linked to the salvation of the world.

13. Thus according to the OT the land forms an essential part of the election by which God has bound himself to this particular people. Certainly the bond of God with his people is not severed when the people are outside the land, and certainly the people can live there also in quiet and peace, but the enforced separation of people and land is always something abnormal. There is no question of a separate election of the land; rather, it is a vital aspect of the election of Israel. This cannot, however, be said of the city of Jerusalem, or of the kingship, or of the independent state. Whatever value may have been attached to them in particular times, they were not inherent in Israel's election. Concerning Jerusalem, the special importance of the city is based on four elements according to the O.T. First, it is the place in which God has chosen to be present in his sanctuary amidst his people. The election of the city (e.g. 1 Kings 8; 2 Kings 21; 2 Chron 6:5) is determined by the fact that God wants his name to be in the temple of Zion. Second, Jerusalem derives its significance from the fact that it is the city of the Davidic kingship since the election of David. Furthermore, in certain OT passages Jerusalem is a symbol for the whole land and the whole people. Finally, there are passages which ascribe to Jerusalem an eschatological significance.

14. Nor was the historical kingship an essential element of the election of OT Israel. The very fact that it came into existence at a relatively late date and amidst strong prophetic criticism is proof of this. This kingship can truly express the sovereignty of God over his people, but it can also be an abandonment of God. Therefore since its beginning it always had a certain ambivalence. And the fact that the people had no state of their own played no decisive role as long as foreign rulers let them live in quiet and peace in their own land and did not prevent them from living according to the order willed by God.

Identity and Alienation

15. According to their own OT witness the Jewish people as a whole were called to be God's covenant people. Their vocation was to realize, as a national entity, in the land given to them for that purpose, a society in which only God's will was law, in order to mediate salvation to all nations. The true identity of Israel as God's people lay in its being determined by its election; it is characterized by three inter-related elements: the reception of God's revelation, the dwelling in the "promised land" in order to form a holy society, and its universal significance.

16. The people in their totality were not faithful to their identity. The prophets vehemently accuse Israel for refusing to listen to God's word when they call it to repentance. Again and again the OT speaks of Israel's defection and disobedience. This mirrors our own alienation from God. Therefore it should be a matter of wonder and gratefulness for all men that the unfaithful people did not lose their vocation as covenant-people. That this did not happen is due to God's election, which cannot be nullified. Therefore Israel still shows signs of its vocation, even in its alienation. God in his election puts his mark upon Israel as his covenant-people, and this is a visible mark.

17. The OT testifies to Israel's alienation; however, simultaneously the book itself is a sign of Israel's identity. For these writings are written in, and have been preserved and collected by, this people, which itself is constantly criticized in them. The very existence of the OT — these books by which the church also lives — is a sign of Israel's vocation to be a blessing to all nations.

18. In respect of content, there is a manifest tension between the true and the false prophets, between those who understood the unique revelation of their unique God and those who confused it with and linked it to their own wishes or the religions of the nations. In the centuries after the Babylonian exile, groups of the pious were formed, who separated themselves from the great masses; in practice this meant that they withdrew from the masses and that they relinquished the idea that in Israel nation and congregation should be identical. And while some held fast to the universal vocation of their people, as particularly the great prophets of former times had expressed it, others wanted to preserve the nation as a holy and separate community, in such a way that they lost sight of this vocation.

III. Jesus, the Jewish People, and the Nations

Continuity and Discontinuity

19.   In the foregoing we have tried to clarify wherein lies the identity of the chosen people, according to their Law and their Prophets. We have seen how their witness was a judgement against Israel and how it pointed to its alienation. But our questions are directed towards the Jewish people of today. Is there continuity with the Israel of the OT? Are the things which were said there still valid for the Jewish people of today? At first sight we might be inclined to give a negative answer. The NT witnesses were so impressed by the immensity and newness of what they had received in Christ, that they seem to leave hardly any room for continuity. Christians in the past have mostly stressed the discontinuity which was the result of the coming of Christ. We, however, intend to bring to the fore particular aspects of the NT which have not played a great role in the church up till now. The difference between the Jewish people and the other peoples is pre-supposed in most parts of the NT, whether explicitly or tacitly. We intend to make this difference fruitful in our thinking about Israel. For we believe that it is imperative to keep in mind that the place which Christ has in the history of Israel is different from the place which he has in the history of the other peoples. For then it will become apparent that the discontinuity in the Jewish people, which is mentioned in the NT, takes place within the framework of the continuity of God's special acting with Israel.

Jesus and the Jewish People

20.   The way in which God acts with the Jewish people in Jesus as their Messiah follows the same lines as the way in which he acted in the history of the O.T. That history shows how God came to his people again and again. To be God's people means that God is with the people. Always anew and always differently he comes in his law and in the words of the prophets. The entire OT witnesses to this Immanuel, to this God-with-Israel. In Jesus God has come anew to his people in a fulness and immediacy formerly unknown; in him Immanuel is present as never before. And just as formerly God did plead with his people by means of the prophets, so now he pleads through Jesus, but yet more urgently and more directly, that they may turn towards him. So God's acting in Jesus Christ confirms his faithfulness to Israel.

21. This is immediately manifest from the speeches of Peter, Stephen and Paul, as they are recorded in the Book of Acts. The Jews are called upon to accept Jesus as Messiah, because he is the continuation and fulfillment of the history of their own people. If they accepted him, they would become what they have been all along in God's view, namely his covenant people. And somehow the coming of the Kingdom of God depends on this acceptance (Acts 3:19,20; Rom 11:25). However, this is such a new and unknown prospect that we cannot know it or describe it; we can only dream of it.

22. The Jewish people as a whole did not pay heed to this call. Just as the NT witnesses saw Jesus' coming in the line of the prophets, so also they saw his rejection by the people. One has only to think of the parable of the unjust tenants in the Gospels and of the speeches in Acts mentioned above. But Jesus is more than the prophets. Therefore the tension already existing in OT times between identity and alienation has obtained its deepest confirmation and utmost accentuation in the rejection of Jesus. In his preaching and his behaviour Jesus radicalized the relation between God and man to such a degree that he confronted man directly with God himself. He addressed especially those Jews who because of their way of life had placed themselves outside the pale of the true people of God. Thus he came into diametrical opposition to the "pious" who tried to ensure and maintain the continued existence of the chosen people by faithful observance of the law. He also repudiated those who wanted to restore national independence and who in this way strove for the self-preservation of their people. The Jewish people as a whole did not accept this renewal of the ancient prophets' criticism. Thereby they confirmed the judgement which these prophets had pronounced against them.

23. We have said that the rejection of Jesus was an extreme radicalization of the alienation of Israel from its true vocation. It may therefore be asked whether this has gone so far that Israel is not only alienated from its true identity but has in fact completely lost it. If this were so, the people would no longer be defined by their vocation to be God's special people after the rejection of Jesus. It was primarily Paul who explicitly posed this question and answered it in the negative. Because God's election is based solely on his own faithfulness, this people remains even now the chosen people, and their sonship and the given promises are still valid.

The Land in the NT
24. If the election of the people and the promises connected with it remain valid, it follows that the tie between people and land also remains by the grace of God. For the chosen people and the land belong essentially together according to the OT.

25. This is not actually expressed in the NT. On the other hand, nothing is to be found there which denies it. Jesus spoke about the destruction of

Jerusalem and the expulsion from the land as judgements on the Jewish people, but this is entirely in line with the prophets' preaching of judgement. This judgement is not a final word; it pre-supposes as its setting the continuing association of the people and the land. Paul, the only one of the NT witnesses who reflected on the place of the Jewish people in the divine plan of salvation after their rejection of Christ, lived in a time when it was still self-evident that the Jews lived in their own land. Therefore there was no reason for him to consider the land as a special question. Even after the fall of Jerusalem the Jews still lived in the land. All NT writers knew the land as the centre of Jewry, even of those large groups which lived abroad. Therefore it is not surprising that — with the possible exception of a few references — the tie between the Jewish people and their land is not mentioned in the N.T. The NT explicitly expresses only that which through and since Christ's coming has been changed. To this the messianic kingship and the place and function of the temple and the cult belonged, and therefore they are mentioned. But because Christ caused no breach in the relation between the people and the land, no reference was made to this. Now that we, many centuries later and in an entirely different situation, read the NT in view of questions which played no role at that time, we need to become aware of its hidden presuppositions.

26. At this point it is necessary to pose the question whether according to the NT Jerusalem still has a special theological function for the people of Israel after Christ. It is clear that the cult and the kingship, which in the OT were both connected with Jerusalem, are fulfilled in Christ in such a way that the exceptional importance of the city can no longer be based upon them. As the symbol of the Jewish people and as the sum of the whole land, however, the city is mentioned also in the N.T. Another question is whether Jerusalem has still a special significance for all people of the world in the eschatological fulfillment. Exploration of this question has hardly started yet.

Jesus and the Nations

27. Jesus Christ has a fundamentally different function for the nations and for Israel. The Jews are called back by him to the God who bound himself to them from their beginning. But the Gentiles are not called back to their origin by Jesus Christ; rather, they are called to something which is radically new in their history. In the proclamation of him as the Messiah of Israel they are confronted with God himself, whom they had not known before. In Christ those who were once far off were given access to him who also was their God.

The Church

28. The Jewish people as a whole did not accept the recall out of their

alienation which their Messiah had urged. This already was clear to Paul and to all other NT writers. But there were individuals among this people who did accept Jesus Christ. In him they recognized the vocation of their people and they placed themselves under his judgement and his acquittal. Thus, vicariously on behalf of their whole people, they attained in him the true nature of God's people. And those of the Gentiles who came to know God in the Messiah of Israel were incorporated into the people of God. This is the church, a unity of Jews and Gentiles in Christ, running through all peoples and nations. Her true identity lies in the following: called as a messianic communion, which represents all men, Jews and non-Jews, she is to depict, in anticipation of the future, the coming universal Kingdom of God, and imitating Jesus she is to stand prophetically and invitingly amidst the Jewish people and the nations, and also over against both of them. Thus for the church also her true nature lies in the vocation to which God has called her.

29. Was the church faithful to her true nature in NT times? In the NT, it is difficult to get an explicit answer; the communion of believers was still in its infancy and could look forward to an open future. Still, in the controversy of Peter and Paul, in the Pauline epistles and in the letters to the seven churches in Asia which form the beginning of the Book of Revelation, indications are to be found that the portrayal of the divine Kingdom in the visibility of the church has been an ambivalent matter from the beginning. Apparently the church has always shown, just as Israel did, signs of alienation beside signs of her identiy.

IV. The Jewish People in our Times

The not yet

30. In Jesus Christ God has come to Jews and non-Jews in a way which cannot be surpassed. In him the final decision is made. Still, we live in a world which has not yet reached its ultimate fulfillment. The Jews did not let themselves be called back by their Messiah to their true identity as God's people. They have continued on the course of alienation which they had already taken before him. And in regard to the nations, even if signs are to be seen in their history of the confrontation with the God of Israel in Jesus Christ, there is no question of a real acceptance of him. The NT writers could still expect that the Gentiles to whom God's salvation in Jesus Christ came after it had come to the Jewish people, would certainly listen (cf Acts 28:28); but to us it has become clear that up till now it is only a small minority which has really listened. And even the church, which is called to live in strength of the salvation it has received in Christ, fulfills its calling only in great imperfection. It is apparent that neither the Jewish people nor the non-Jews have reached their destiny willed by God. History still goes on. That is divine judgement and at the same time the grace of God's preserving faithfulness and love. Man continues to exist.

31. In the final fulfillment the difference between Jews and Gentiles will no longer play any role, because God will be all in all; but as this fulfillment has not yet come, the Jewish people can continue to exist in their particularity. This is the eminent sign of God's preserving faithfulness and love. The situation of the people of Israel regarding salvation is the same as it was in NT times. They are still, even in their alienation, the special people to which God has bound himself. Their election remains valid; and through this election they are determined and marked.

Visible Reality

32. The people about which we are talking are a historical datum. One can ask who exactly belongs to it, what ultimately is a Jew, and whether the name of "people", which is used for other peoples, can strictly speaking be applied here. In any case it is certain that the Jews themselves know that they belong together: a feeling of solidarity links them to each other, be they believers or non-believers, Zionists or anti-Zionists, Israeli or of another nationality. Through this belonging together, experienced by themselves through the ages and recognizable also to non-Jews, it appears that the Jewish people are still an existing and visible fact. And to this people God has decided to bind himself in such a way that all they do or suffer affects himself somehow. All they do or suffer can become to us a sign of him. That is true even when the Jews themselves deny it and want to be like other men and peoples. In the Jewish people we are always dealing with God himself. Could that perhaps be the reason that the more this people comes visibly to the fore in history, the more it gives offence?

Alienation and Identity

33. In the past Christians used to pay the most attention to those aspects of the Jewish people which showed most clearly their alienation from God and their destiny. And indeed, judged by the three connected elements which, as said above, are characteristic for Israel's identity as God's people, its present-day alienation is manifest. The people as a whole feel themselves no longer bound to God and his revelation: there are believing and unbelieving Jews. The oneness of people and congregation exists no longer. The vocation to be a separate, special people for the sake of the other peoples is denied by many. And the tie based merely upon the divine promise which binds people and land together is in our time often misunderstood as a purely historical or nationalistic claim. If we compare the existing reality with the true character of the Jewish people as professed in the OT, and as confirmed by Jesus Christ, we understand the image used by Paul, namely that they are like branches broken off.

34. We should however not stress this alienation so emphatically and onesidedly, that we forget that the Jews are still the chosen people. As such they are a sign of God's faithfulness. This sign is primarily seen in the fact that they still exist; the Jewish people cannot be done away with. Even in their alienation their true nature can still be recognized. To keep to the image of Paul, it is true that the branches are broken off, but they remain branches which show that they properly belong to the cultivated olive tree. That is to say, there are still signs to be seen of the true identity of the Jewish people. But because it is identity in alienation, these signs are extremely ambivalent,

35. In the first place we must point to the observance of the law by orthodox Jews. They want to regulate their whole life in all its details by the revealed will of God. This observance more than anything else has preserved the Jewish people in their special character throughout the ages. Nevertheless this faithfulness to the law is ambivalent. It easily becomes a means of moral self-assertion. It is but a small step from loyalty towards God's commandments to legalism. Because of their zeal for the law the Jews have rejected Jesus. To such a degree the maintenance and the loss of identity are apparently intertwined.

36. We see a sign of the true nature of the people also in their relation to the land. This too has played a preserving role through the ages. The feeling of relatedness has never been lost entirely, although in the last century many Jews have denied it. But those who believed in the special vocation of the people have always stressed that dispersion among the nations, without a centre of their own in the promised land, was not in accordance with the final destiny of their people. In our time the longing for the land has shown itself as a power which shapes history. This longing has received visible form in the return of many Jews. This return partakes of the ambivalence of identity and alienation. One part of the Zionists wanted merely a home, anywhere in the world. But this could be realized only in the land of Palestine, and this can be a sign to us that the special tie with the land, made by God's election, remains valid even when the Jews do not recognize it.

37. Among the factors which have kept the Jews together throughout the centuries we have mentioned their observance of the law and their relatedness to the land of Palestine. In addition, as a third factor, anti-Semitism has also served to keep them together. It is of such a totally different order from the first-mentioned factors that it seems nearly nonsensical to compare them in any way. Nevertheless, in spite of our utter abhorrence of it, we dare to see even here a pointer to the identity of Israel. The Jews who live amidst the nations are a summons to the conscience of these nations to safeguard the rights of all men. Where a nation is in danger of sinking into racism or into national self-glorification, one of the first warning-signs is that the Jews are felt to be offensive. For however much they may have tried to adapt themselves, and however many attempts may have been made to assimilate them to their surroundings, they remain a distinctive element in the national body. In the very fact that they are time and again an annoyance and a stumbling block, they fulfill — we have to

say, in spite of themselves — their universal vocation: they are a touchstone for the humaneness and righteousness of other men. This is not all that could be said about the complex phenomenon of anti-Semitism, but we are convinced that it certainly is one of its aspects.

38. However, this universal vocation which belongs to the nature of the Jewish people, does not only show in the offence they give. It is often pointed out that in the struggle for justice and humaneness a remarkably large number of Jews is found. In this fact also we see, in secularized form, evidence of the destiny of the Jewish people to be a blessing to the other peoples.

The Church as Reflection of Israel

39. Whenever the church forgets that the Jews are preserved in their particularity as chosen people — by the grace of God, she jeopardizes her own existence. For up till now the church has not made good her destiny any more than has the Jewish people. Though she is essentially the messianic oneness of Jews and Gentiles, she appears mostly as a church of the non-Jews. She has forgotten her origin to such a degree that she considers the few Jewish Christians in her midst strange exceptions with whom she does not know what to do. Again and again the nationalistic self-assertion, to which the Jewish people now, as in the time of Jesus, are in danger of falling victim, has become equally the sin of Christians. And the same thing can be said of the moralism and legalism into which the observance of the law has often degenerated among the Jews.

40. Nevertheless, the church does not cease to be the church of Jesus Christ. Of this fact too we see the visible signs: she proclaims God's coming to man in judgement and acquittal, administers baptism and celebrates the Lord's Supper, and many of her members fight for peace and justice. But it is only thanks to God's electing faithfulness that the church is maintained in her identity notwithstanding her alienation — the same faithfulness of which the Jewish people in their own way are a visible sign to us.

V. The State of Israel

The Significance of the Return

41. We have spoken about the unique destiny of the Jews to be God's covenant people and about the unique tie which binds them and the land of Palestine together. Even the rejection of Jesus Christ did not bring any change in this regard. Thereby the people have indeed affirmed their alienation which they had shown already, but they are still the chosen people, destined to fulfil a lasting and separate role. In our time many Jews have again gone to the land of Palestine. In this way the people, who were threatened with disappearance, partly through assimilation, partly through awful pogroms and acts of extermination, have again obtained a new, clearly visible form. Precisely in its concrete visibility, this return points to the special significance of this people in the midst of the nations, and to the saving faithfulness of God; it is a sign for us that it is God's will to be on earth together with man. Therefore we rejoice in this reunion of people and land.

42. However, we do not intend to imply that the return is the final stage of history, nor that the people can never again be expelled from the land. Indeed, in the return the grace of God's lasting election has become manifest, but this return carries with it a special threat. For it could be that the other peoples deny a place to the Jews who are in their midst. It could also be that Israel does not use the new chance which it has received to fulfill its destiny in the land. But both these perils cannot prevent us from understanding the return positively as a confirmation of God's lasting purpose with his people.

The relative Necessity of the State

43. However, the issue is not merely the return but also the state. God's promise applies to the lasting tie of people and land, but not in the same way to the tie of people and state. In biblical times the Jewish people have lived for centuries in Palestine without having an independent state of their own. It is also possible that in the future circumstances will be such that the Jews as an entity can live unhindered in their land without forming a specifically Jewish state, or even that they can fulfill their vocation better if they are part of a larger whole. But as matters are at the moment, we see a free state as the only possibility which safeguards the existence of the people and which offers them the chance to be truly themselves. The former hope of some for a bi-national state in the full sense of the word, seems in the present situation not possible to realize. For right after the Second World War a great influx of Jewish refugees disrupted the precarious equilibrium of Jews and Arabs. It is still necessary for the land to offer refuge to all Jews all over the world. That seems to preclude the possibility of a bi-national state, at least for the moment, to say nothing of the existing hostility between Arabs and Jews. Another possibility, which is sometimes mentioned, that of a federation in Palestine, presupposes at least that peace should first be made. Finally there is the possibility which the Arab countries offer the Jews, namely to accept a minority position in a Muslim state. But this would imply that in the promised land the Jewish ghetto with its attendant mentality and dangers would be continued. Therefore we are convinced that everyone who accepts the reunion of the Jewish people and the land for reasons of faith, has also to accept that in the given circumstances the people should have a state of their own.

The State and the special Place of the Jewish People

44. Because of the special place of the Jewish people we endorse in the present situation the right of existence of the State of Israel. On the other hand we wonder whether this same special place does not also make this right questionable. First of all, we remember the way in which the State came into existence in 1948. This took place in a human, all too human way, as is the case with practically every other state; all kinds of political means and often means of violence have been used. But the Jewish people have never been better than other peoples. The entry in the land under Joshua and the return under Nehemia were, morally speaking, dubious affairs too. The special place of Israel was never based on its moral qualities, but solely on what in the OT is called God's righteousness, that is his unmerited, steadfast covenant-love. This love can never be a license to sin. But it is not annulled by sin either. Therefore we ought not to dispute on moral grounds the right of the State of Israel to exist. Otherwise we would have to ask ourselves how we ourselves can stand before God.

45. In the second place we must ask whether the universal purpose of Israel's election does not exclude the possibility of a state of their own. Indeed, the state carries with it the temptation for this people to become a nation like the other nations. The existence of a state can easily lead to an attitude of isolation, rivalry and defensiveness; and if this took place, then Israel could not fulfil its calling to be a bridge between separate peoples (Is 19:23-25). But this far from imaginary danger is not necessarily inherent in the existence of a state. A state means concentration and structuralization of national life, but not necessarily isolation. In the present situation at least, a state gives greater opportunity to the Jews to fulfil their vocation than any alternative can offer.

46. Therefore we maintain that whoever accepts for the Jewish people a role of their own among the nations must also in view of the political problems in and around Palestine accept for this people the right to a state of their own. Because this acceptance is based on the lasting tie with the land in virtue of the promise, i.e. because it is ultimately based on reasons of faith, it cannot be a matter of *uncommitted* discussion in the Christian community. Otherwise one takes the risk of divorcing the NT from the OT, God from history, and his commandment from his promise; that would mean a de-spiritualization and de-moralization of the Christian faith.

The Vocation and the Ambiguity of the State

47. Because of the special place in which by divine decree the Jews stand, the State of Israel also has a dimension of its own. The election of the people implies the vocation to realize their peoplehood in an exemplary way. Therefore, the State also has to be exemplary. Israel is called to live in its State in such a manner that a new understanding of what a state is, is enacted before the eyes of the other peoples. But those who among Israel

plead for this exemplary existence find little response at the present time. In the State also there is manifest the brokenness and ambiguity to which the entire history of the Jewish people witnesses.

48. The land is given to Israel as dwelling place; there it can have its state. But the boundaries of this state cannot be read from the Bible. The territory in which the Jewish people lived in OT times has had very different boundaries, and these never coincided with those of which the prophetic promises spoke. The only thing of which we are sure is that these boundaries must be such that they offer the Jewish people a dwelling place where they can be themselves. But it is a matter of a dwelling place, not a sphere of power and control. The necessity of protecting their dwelling place should not induce the Jews to make it into a nationalistic state in which the only thing that counts is military power. It is true that the so-called Christian states also have frequently succumbed to this temptation. But this is exactly the point, namely that in this way Israel is in danger of becoming a people like all other peoples, not worse and not better. Such a collective assimilation would be a denial of its true nature.

49. The Jewish people are called to exercise justice in an exemplary way. This too is an essential aspect of their true identity. In this respect the problems caused by the founding of the State of Israel and its later military victories are a particular challenge for the people. Hundreds of thousands of Palestinian refugees live miserably, without rights, around the borders of Israel. It belongs to Israel's vocation that it should know itself to be responsible for them and that it should do all it can to put right the injustice done to them. This is possible only if it were to search for a political solution which would not be based on violence, as is mostly the case among the other peoples, but which would be based on justice and true humanity.

50. According to the biblical witness God promised the land to his people at a time when other peoples lived there. Israel could never lay claim to the land by right. It was not allowed to consider it as its own possession. It had to learn, and to show others, what it means to live in a land by the grace of God. Hence comes the OT commandment to treat the foreigner in its midst as if he were a fellow Jew. Now, in our own time, Israel is offered the chance to establish a form of government which guarantees its own Jewish existence, and which at the same time respects the full freedom and dignity of its non-Jewish fellow citizens. But in spite of rights which are officially granted, these non-Jewish people are actually treated as second class citizens. It may be true that at the moment weighty reasons of political expediency can be given for this discrimination. But it is not in accordance with Israel's calling.

Jerusalem

51. Through its specific development Jerusalem offers Israel an outstanding opportunity to practice a new, non-nationalistic and non-exclusive way of thinking. This city, which because of its history has great meaning for many Christians and Muslims, ought to be a kind of experimental garden where various nations may live together in peace. But as soon as we state this, questions arise which we cannot answer unanimously. Has the city become the concentrated expression of the union of land and people to such a degree that, if by reason of faith one supports the right of Israel to live in its land, one also has to include an affirmation of the lasting tie between this people and its city? Or can the exemplary function of Jerusalem as a city of peace, to which all nations can go up, be realized fully only if the city were internationalized and made independent of all other states? Or should one plead for a status of its own for Jerusalem within Israel, in order that around this city the State may develop into a state which is really a blessing for all nations and states? We have no clear and unanimous answer to these questions. But we believe that the problems concerning the city of Jerusalem call for a solution by Israel in a new framework of political thinking.

Election as Calling and as Offence

52. In speaking of Israel's unfaithfulness to its special calling, we did not suppose that we are better than the Jews. We are only too conscious of the fact that we too as Christians, as churches, as so-called Christian states have repeatedly been guilty of discrimination, inhumanity and impermissible forms of nationalism. If Israel were a state like other states, we would not judge it by standards which no other state meets. But we believe that Israel is unique: its nature is based on God's election, for the Jews are still that special people which by God's promises is tied to this particular land. Therefore we expect from this people more than we expect from any other people. He who is placed in a special position has to act in a special manner.

53. Many Jews are not at all eager to be placed in an exceptional position and to have to solve the problems which the State of Israel poses, in a way to which the other peoples do not yet live up. And indeed, their special position has often seemed offensive to the Jews themselves. In view of what has been said above about identity and alienation this can hardly be surprising. But even when the Jewish people in their public life do not yet really meet the demands of their destiny, we are not justified in rejecting the right of existence of their State. For that right is based on God's preserving the identity of his people even in their alienation, and on his dealing with them in a special way.

VI. Epilogue

Church and Israel

54. Israel's way through history is interconnected with the expectation of

the church and, therefore, as Christians we cannot be silent about Israel. The full realization of the identity of Israel would mean that the Jewish people would truly accept God's coming in their midst. But this would be the same thing as to accept Jesus Christ as the one in whom God has affirmed and fulfilled the covenant with his people. The actual acceptance of Christ would open the way to the complete fulfillment of God's purpose with the world, to the Kingdom of God, in which the difference between Jews and Gentiles would be no longer of any account. But as long as we still live in a transitional state, this side of the fulfillment, God will preserve, side by side with the church, the Jewish people as a visible sign of his electing faithfulness.

55. In this time before the ultimate fulfillment, we as the church are called together with the people of Israel to be true to our vocation. The difference between us is that our starting point is the way of Jesus Christ, who is not yet recognized by Israel as the fulfillment of *its* destiny. But we ourselves also do not live truly and entirely on the basis of the salvation which we have received. Indeed, if we were to live in that way, the Jews would be made jealous. The fact that does not happen, shows how imperfectly the church fulfills her calling; the criticism which we make against the Jewish people comes back upon our own heads. The Christian church too has not yet reached her destiny, she too lives still in a transitional state. The Jewish people and the church are both travellers and both are preserved, each in its own way, in God's faithfulness.

The following statement was submitted to the executive committee of the Lutheran Council in the U.S.A. in April 1971, and transmitted to the presidents of the three bodies participating in the co-operative agency, Lutheran Church of America, Lutheran Church Missouri Synod, and American Lutheran Church.

Improved relationships among separated Christian churches in recent decades have also led to growing conversation between Jewish and Christian groups. We commend all endeavors which seek greater understanding, mutual confidence, elimination of tensions, and cooperation in the quest for justice and peace, and note statements issued by Lutheran groups which are helpful in these areas.

Amid the pluralism of American society today and in the face of many practical problems facing Christians, Jews, and all men of goodwill, it is especially necessary to foster and expand such conversations on more local levels, as a contribution to community understanding and cooperation, to heal wounds of the past, and to understand better our common heritage and common humanity. Today the mission of the church surely includes such conversations, and indeed must often begin with them. We urge

Lutheran pastors, people, and institutions to seek greater involvements in such endeavors.

The Christian cannot fully understand what it means to be Jewish but our common ground in humanity and in the Hebrew Scriptures makes a base for beginning. In order to have authentic relationships there must be honesty, openness, frankness, and mutual respect along with a recognition of the real differences that exist and a willingness to risk confronting these differences.

To these ends we offer some practical suggestions and make some observations as to methods so that conversations may be both honest and fruitful:

1.   In localities where Lutherans are comparatively few in number, they are encouraged to cooperate with other Christian groups in initiating and sustaining conversation with Jews.

2.   Where Lutherans comprise a substantial group within a locality, they are encouraged to take the initiative in fostering conversation and community understanding.

3.   Meetings should be jointly planned so as to avoid any suspicion of proselytizing and to lessen the danger of offense through lack of sensitivity or accurate information about the other group.

4.   Because of the long history of alienation between the two groups, Christians and Jews should remember that one meeting does little more than set the stage for serious conversations. False hopes and superficial optimism by either group can lead to despair and further alienation.

5.   On both sides, living communities of faith and worship are involved. Because of fervent commitments, emotions may run deep. It should be underscored that neither polemics nor conversions are the aim of such conversations, nor is false irenicism or mere surface agreement. There may remain honest differences, even as broad areas of agreement are discovered.

6.   If we have been open and have shared our assumptions, prejudices, traditions and convictions, we may be able to share in realistic goal setting, especially in regard to further understanding and common cause in spiritual and social concerns such as fostering human rights.

7.   Different methods of procedure may be followed as mutually determined locally, such as:

    a) Educational visits to advance mutual understanding of artistic, liturgical tradition.

    b) Exchange visits at regular worship services, "open houses", and special celebrations, followed by explanation and discussion.

    c) Informal small group discussions in homes in the manner of the "living room dialogues". Participants may involve one synagogue and one congregation or neighborhood groups without regard to membership.

d) Weekend retreats with equal participation of members from both groups and equality of expertise.

e) Popular lectures, discussions, and demonstrations by well-informed resource persons. Lutherans might invite representatives of the American Jewish Committee, Jewish Chautauqua Society, Anti-Defamation League of B'nai B'rith, National Conference of Christians and Jews, and Jewish theological schools.

f) Scholarly lectures and discussions by experts in biblical, historical and theological studies.

8.   Possible topics include: Our common heritage; the people of God and Covenant; Christian and Jewish views of man; the significance of Hebrew Scriptures today; law, righteousness and justice; State of Israel; the Christian Church in Israel; survey of the attitudes and teachings of the Church concerning Judaism; the image of the Jew in Christian literature; Luther and the Jews; the meaning of suffering; can a Hebrew Christian be a Jew? an Israeli?; eschatology in Christian and Jewish theology; the significance of the Septuagint; the universal God in an age of pluralism; the state and the religious community in Jewish and Lutheran traditions; what can we do together?

9.   Christians should make it clear that there is no biblical or theological basis for anti-Semitism. Supposed theological or biblical bases for anti-Semitism are to be examined and repudiated. Conscious or unconscious manifestations of discrimination are to be opposed.

The Metropolitan New York Synod of the Lutheran Church in America adopted a statement on the writings of Martin Luther. September 1971.

The statement

a) repudiates the anti-Semitic writings of Dr. Martin Luther;
b) admits that anti-Semitism exists among Christians today;
c) contains a commitment to "repudiate and actively oppose" every form of anti-Semitism.

A Resolution on anti-Semitism, adopted at the North Carolina State Baptist Convention in 1971, was followed by a similar resolution passed by the Southern Baptist Convention in 1972.

Whereas, anti-Semitism has been a serious problem for the Church through most of Christian history, and
Whereas, this unchristian attitude on the part of many people led to brutal persecution of the Jews in numerous countries and societies, and

Whereas, the most flagrant and cruel expression of this spiritual malignancy, the Nazi holocaust, transpired in our generation, and
Whereas, latent anti-Semitism lies barely under the surface in many Western, Christian cultures today, and
Whereas, many Christian communions and denominations, including our own, have failed to take a sufficiently vigorous stand against anti-Semitism, and
Whereas, it is clearly a moral and ethical question of the greatest magnitude, and
Whereas, Baptists share with Jews a heritage of persecution and suffering for conscience's sake,

Therefore, be it *Resolved* that this Convention go on record as opposed to any and all forms of anti-Semitism; that it declare anti-Semitism unchristian; that we messengers to this Convention pledge ourselves to combat anti-Semitism in every honorable, Christian way,
Be it further *Resolved* that Southern Baptists covenant to work positively to replace all anti-Semitic bias with the Christian attitude and practice of love for Jews who, along with other men, are equally beloved of God.

The Lutheran World Federation—Commission on Studies,
Geneva, Switzerland, 1971.
Guidelines for the Furtherance of the Study of
the Church and the Jewish People.

The Commission on Studies of the Lutheran World Federation recognizes the importance and urgency of the continuing study in the member churches and by the Federation of questions dealing with the Church and the Jewish People. The Commission sees this as a particular responsibility for the Lutheran churches.

The Commission on Studies sees its work in this field being done along three lines:

1) The furtherance of study work in the member churches and between member churches, collaboration to be sought with other churches and specialized institutes;

2) cooperation with the World Council of Churches;

3) consultations or conferences for evaluation of the study work and the exploration of basic theological and methodological questions.

1.　It is our opinion that the life of the Lutheran Church in Israel should be dealt with as a continuing concern by the Department and Commission on Church Cooperation, the question of the legal situation of Christians in Israel being dealt with also by the General Secretariat.
2.　Questions of anti-Semitism and Christian literature, or publications

and films on Jewish-Christian relations, etc. should remain basically the responsibility of the member churches.

Staff of the Department of Studies will be glad to see to it that information channels are open between those working on Jewish-Christian questions in the various member churches, so that there can be direct contact and cooperation if desired, with a desk in the Department responsible for this field.

The reports of the Løgumkloster Consultation held in 1964 and of the former Committee on the Church and the Jews should be sent to selected individuals, institutes and groups in the member churches with the request to give them careful scrutiny and to send their findings to the Department.

The following questions should receive attention in reaction to the documents: What are the strengths and weaknesses of the reports? Where are the open questions? At what points has too facile an answer been given? Are there basic theological or methodological questions to be raised? How are the proposals for further study to be judged?

The Commission on Studies encourages staff of the Department to intensify and extend cooperation with relevant staff of the World Council of Churches to draw Lutheran groups working on questions related to the church and the Jews into closer ecumenical collaboration at the various levels. Staff of the WCC should be asked to help plan any conferences or consultations. Staff of the Department is requested to respond, if possible, to any requests for assistance that may come from the WCC.

The Commission will call a Consultation on the Church and the Jewish People in 1972 or 1973. It should include representatives from the groups working on this question in the member churches, other experts and, if possible, persons from the Middle East. It may be desirable to invite individual Jews to present their views and insights. The responses of the groups in the churches should be taken into account in identifying the issues to be discussed at the consultation. The groups should be asked, where possible, to cover the expenses of their representatives to the Consultation.

The Commission has asked the Consultant on Mission Studies, Dr. Martin Luther Kretzmann, to bear staff responsibility for contact with the groups in the member churches and for planning the consultation. A full report on plans for the consultation will come before the Commission at its next meeting. It is the hope of the Commission that the consultation will stimulate further work on the question of dialogue between Jews and Christians and on Christian-Jewish relations and identify specific issues for continuing study in the churches.

It is this engagement on the local level which is the aim of study work by the Commission on Studies in this field. For it is on the local level where good Christian-Jewish relations become manifest, where existential dialogue takes place, where witness is made and where solidarity is shown. It is also engagement on the local level which qualifies and equips a person for international study and for dialogue between representatives of the world-wide Jewish community and representative Christians, as is being carried out by the World Council of Churches. The work of the LWF should be to strengthen this engagement at both levels.

Some Observations and Guidelines for Conversations between Lutherans and Jews

Improved relationships among separated Christian churches in recent decades have also led to growing conversation between Jewish and Christian groups. We commend all endeavours which seek greater understanding, mutual confidence, eliminations of tensions, and cooperation in the quest for justice and peace, and note statements issued by Lutheran groups which are helpful in these areas.

Amid the pluralism of American society today and in the face of many practical problems facing Christians, Jews, and all men of good will, it is especially necessary to foster and expand such conversations on more local levels, as a contribution to community understanding and cooperation, to heal wounds of the past, and to understand better our common heritage and common humanity. Today the mission of the church surely includes such conversations, and indeed must often begin with them. We urge Lutheran pastors, people, and institutions to seek greater involvement in such endeavours.

The Christian cannot fully understand what it means to be Jewish but our common ground in humanity and in the Hebrew Scriptures makes a base for beginning. In order to have authentic relationships there must be honesty, openness, frankness, and mutual respect along with a recognition of the real differences that exist and a willingness to risk confronting these differences.

To these ends we offer some practical suggestions and make some observations as to methods so that conversation may be both honest and fruitful.

1.   In localities where Lutherans are comparatively few in number, they are encouraged to cooperate with other Christian groups in initiating and sustaining conversation with Jews.

2.   Where Lutherans comprise a substantial group within a locality, they are encouraged to take the initiative in fostering conversation and community understanding.

3.   Meetings should be jointly planned so as to avoid any suspicion of proselytizing and to lessen the danger of offense through lack of sensitivity or accurate information about the other group.

4.   Because of the long history of alienation between the two groups, Christians and Jews should remember that one meeting does little more than set the stage for serious conversations. False hopes and superficial optimism by either group can lead to despair and further alienation.

5.   On both sides, living communities of faith and worship are involved.

Because of fervent commitments emotions may run deep. It should be underscored that neither polemics nor conversions are the aim of such conversations, nor is false irenicism or mere surface agreement. There may remain honest differences, even as broad areas of agreement are discovered.
6. If we have been open and have shared our assumptions, prejudices, traditions, and convictions we may be able to share in realistic goal setting, especially in regard to further understanding and common cause in spiritual and social concerns such as fostering human rights.
7. Different methods of procedure may be followed as mutually determined locally, such as:

a) Educational visits to advance mutual understanding of artistic, liturgical tradition.
b) Exchange of visits at regular worship services, "open houses", and special celebrations, followed by explanation and discussion.
c) Informal small group discussions in homes in the manner of the "living-room dialogues". Participants may involve one synagogue and one congregation or neighborhood groups without regard to membership.
d) Week-end retreats with equal participation of members from both groups and equality of expertise.
e) Popular lectures, discussion, and demonstrations by well-informed resource persons. Lutherans might invite representatives of the American Jewish Committee, Jewish Chautauqua Society, Anti-Defamation League of B'nai B'rith, National Conference of Christians and Jews, and Jewish theological schools.
f) Scholarly lectures and discussions by experts in biblical, historical, and theological studies.

8. Possible topics include: Our Common Heritage; The People of God and Covenant; Christian and Jewish Views of Man; The Significance of Hebrew Scriptures Today; Law, Righteousness and Justice; State of Israel; The Christian Church in Israel; Survey of the Attitudes and Teachings of the Church concerning Judaism; The Image of the Jew in Christian Literature; Luther and the Jews; The Meaning of Suffering; Can a Hebrew Christian be a Jew? An Israeli?; Eschatology in Christian and Jewish Theology; The Significance of the Septuagint; The Universal God in an Age of Pluralism; The State and the Religious Community in Jewish and Lutheran Traditions; What Can We Do Together?
9. Christians should make it clear that there is no biblical or theological basis for anti-Semitism. Supposed theological or biblical bases for anti-Semitism are to be examined and repudiated. Conscious or unconscious manifestations of discrimination are to be opposed.

The General Conference of The United Methodist Church issued the following Statement on Interreligious Dialogue between Jews and Christians. Atlanta, Ga., 1972.

Common Roots

1. The United Methodist Church understands itself to be a part of the People of God and specifically a part of the whole Christian Church, the Body of Christ. It also gives thanks for its roots in historic Judaism. It rejoices in the reciprocal patrimony of the Old and New Testaments.

The heritage and hopes of an Israel in the context of which Jesus labored have continued to live in the Jewish faith and people. Christian awareness of indebtedness, however, to that history and its relationship to God is not as clear as it ought to be. Not only is the God we worship the same and many of our ethical concerns are held in common, but there are also numerous traditions in Israel's history whose impact upon and potential for the Christian Church were lost or are still undiscovered. Moreover, to be faithful to Jesus the Jew, the contemporary relationship of United Methodist Christians and those who worship as Jews should not be neglected.

Appreciation for common roots should not blind us to the fundamental and inherently mutual theological problems to be faced. The relationship between the covenant of God with Israel and the covenant made in Jesus Christ and the understanding by Jew and Christian of each of these covenants merits exploration anew. Openness to the blessing of God on all covenanted people may lead to useful penetration of the intricacies of the interfaith discussions, if not to ultimate solutions. Serious new conversations need not and should not require either Jews or Christians to sacrifice their convictions. There is rich opportunity for potential growth in mutual understanding.

Service for Humanity

2. At this moment in history, the potential of our common heritage is particularly important for the advancement of causes decisive for the survival of all mankind. While it is true that the concept of human brotherhood and solidarity is not represented by Jews or Christians alone, this concept has been central for both from their beginnings. The sacredness of persons as God's creation is expressed clearly in both the Old and New Testaments. The biblical view of each human being as an intrinsic member of the community of persons forbids any suppression of groups through society at large and any manipulation of individuals as well. Nevertheless, Jews in particular have been victims of systematic oppression and injustice more recurrently and more barbarously than have Christians. Therefore, in order to continue Jewish and Christian efforts for the common cause of mankind, it is not enough for contemporary Christians to be aware of our common origins. Christians must also become aware of that history in which they have deeply alienated the Jews. They are obligated to examine their own implicit and explicit responsibility for the discrimination against and for organized extermination of Jews, as in the recent past. The persecution by Christians of Jews throughout centuries calls for clear repentance and resolve to repudiate past injustice and to seek its elimination in the present. In provision of guidelines for action and in specific processes of reconciling action for all men there is an opportunity now to join hands with Jews in common cause for a human community.

For Jew and Christian alike, God is active in history. The political and social orders are not free from His judgment. Dialogue which does not blink at differences of assumptions and interpretations of Scripture and faith, but which accentuates the fundamental agreement for the sake of service to society can be, in the Providence of God, a timely and fruitful interreligious adventure.

Exploring Together

3. In many areas of spiritual and intellectual concern the past relationship of Jews and Christians has been vitiated by inadequate communication. We have talked past one another instead of with each other. In new conversations there is an important opportunity to move past the polemical use of Scripture and to explore how and why past conditioning keeps us apart, while we have much in common. In such dialogues, an aim of religious or political conversion, or of proselytizing, cannot be condoned.

To commend the love of God in Jesus Christ through saving word and serving work is an ingredient of dialogue for Christians, but anti-Semitism (against Jew or Arab) represents a denial of the love we proclaim and compromises our service of justice. Fruitful discussions should proceed with the clear acknowledgement that there is no valid biblical or theological basis for anti-Semitism. Prejudice and discrimination on racial grounds are not valid expressions of Christian faith. Why people still violate their unity given in God, and in His creation and redemption, should be examined in company with our Jewish brothers and sisters.

Responsibility in Problem Areas

4. Dialogues presently are complicated by problems of scriptural interpretation, conditioned attitudes, and turbulent political struggles such as the search for Jewish and Arab security and dignity in the Middle East. Facing these difficulties together may lead to creative results. In this process, we are obligated to respect the right of the Jews, as of all religious groups, to interpret their own Scriptures with regard to their peoplehood and destiny. When rival political positions each claim scriptural warrant, however, the issues no longer are related simply to religious freedom for one or another but to the political issue of how resources may be distributed justly. In Jewish-Christian dialogue is placed a responsibility for being concerned with the implications of peace and justice for all persons.

The Christian obligation to those who survived the Nazi Holocaust, the understanding of the relationship of land and peoplehood, and the conviction that God loves all persons, suggest that a new dimension in dialogue with Jews is needed. A new perspective for Christians is a prerequisite for the reduction of mutual ignorance and distrust.

Guidelines for Conversations

5.   The principles which have been outlined above implicitly or explicitly suggest some practical guidelines which can instruct conversations in local communities and at other points of interaction. An incomplete list of the more important considerations is attempted here.

a) Wherever possible, conversations with members of Jewish communities should be initiated and maintained through an existing or an *ad hoc* ecumenical framework. The ecumenical body could begin by accepting the principles in this United Methodist statement as a foundation for the dialogue, or by drafting its own.

b) In the absence of cooperative Christian efforts to explore mutual understanding, tensions, and difficulties, United Methodist initiative (or response to Jewish initiative) is to be encouraged.

c) Christian participants should make clear that they do not justify past injustice done by Christians to Jews and that there is no tenable biblical or theological base for anti-Semitism, and that they themselves wish to be free of it.

d) Joint planning of conversations should emphasize the broad purposes of dialogues and lessen suspicion that conversion is a deliberate intention.

e) Honest differences should be expected and probed seriously, even as areas of agreement and mutual support are discovered.

f) A series of meetings with some guarantee of continuity of participants is necessary for fruitful conversation. False hopes and superficial optimism resulting from a single session together can lead to despair and further alienation.

g) The joint study of that part of our tradition which both groups have in common, the Jewish Bible or the Christian Old Testament, can be of paramount importance. It is here that the foundation of Jewish and Christian existence coincide. A joint study has potential for new insight into our mutual relationship and our togetherness.

h) Conversations which begin exploration of scriptural and traditional heritages may move to political, sociological, and economic investigations and might well result in common action in the causes of human rights.

i) The dialogues should not overlook the rich opportunities afforded in visitation of synagogues and churches and in common prayer and other interreligious services.

Declaration of Intent

6. No one can foresee with absolute clarity the shape of the future. Openness to dialogue with other major religions of the world is not excluded for the future, but a bond of understanding and peace between Jew and Christian surely is one key ingredient of a viable community of persons. In both theological and practical issues of the moment there are offered challenges and opportunities for growth.

A reduction of Jewish or Christian beliefs to a tepid lowest common denominator of hardly distinguishable culture religions is not sought in this process. A new confrontation of our common roots, of our common potential for service to humanity, with the benefits from mutual explorations, and with the knotty contemporary problems of world peace commends itself to us. Thus, it is the desire of The United Methodist Church honestly and persistently to participate in conversations with Jews.

Our intent includes commitment to their intrinsic worth and import for society. It includes as well the Christian hope that the "oneness given in Jesus Christ" may become an example of hope for the oneness of humanity. Within this framework and in acknowledgement of the common Fatherhood of God, on all occasions for this new interreligious adventure The United Methodist Church seeks to be responsive.

The General Conference of The United Methodist Church adopted a Declaration on the Rights of Religious Minorities. Atlanta, Ga., 1972.

Religious persecution has been common in the history of civilization. We urge policies and practices that insure the right of every religious group to exercise its faith free from legal, political, or economic restrictions. In particular, we condemn anti-Semitism in both its overt and covert forms, and assert the right of all religions and their adherents to freedom from legal, economic, and social discrimination.

The General Conference of The United Methodist Church adopted a Resolution on the Formation of Mandatory Ecumenical and Interreligious Conference Commissions. Atlanta, Ga., 1972.

The Resolution makes it mandatory "to stimulate understanding and conversations with all Christian bodies, to encourage continuing dialogue with Jewish faith communities, and to encourage an openness of mind toward and an understanding of other major world religions"; and "to stimulate conference, district and congregational participation in councils, conferences, or federations of churches, in interfaith studies and in the use of jointly approved curriculum resources."

The Church and the Jewish People. Report on a Consultation held under the auspices of the Lutheran World Federation. Neuendettelsau, Germany, 1973.

The Commission on Studies laid down the following lines of work:

1) The furtherance of study work in the member churches and between member churches, collaboration to be sought with other churches and specialized institutes;
2) Cooperation with the World Council of Churches;
3) Consultations or conferences for evaluation of the study work and the exploration of basic theological and methodological questions.

A desk in the Department of Studies was made responsible "to see to it that information channels are open between those working on Jewish-Christian questions in the various member churches, so that there can be direct contact and cooperation if desired."

The report of the Logumkloster Consultation and other documents produced by the Standing Committee were sent to the member churches for their comments and evaluation with a view to discover those areas which needed further study.

The Commission on Studies saw the possibility that a Consultation of concerned persons and representatives of study groups might be necessary in the near future. It expressed the hope "that the Consultation will stimulate further work on the question of dialogue between Jews and Christians and Christian-Jewish relations and identify specific issues for continuing study in the churches." Such a Consultation was authorized by the Commission for 1973. Its aim was to be the furtherance of engagement on the local level, "where good Christian-Jewish relations become manifest, where existential dialogue takes place, where witness is made and where solidarity is shown."

Within the framework of the above guidelines, staff of the Department of Studies made contact with various study groups and laid plans for a consultation whose main aim was to deal with methodology, to bring together persons engaged in various study programs and dialogues with the aim of exchanging information, defining areas of study and suggesting ways in which the Lutheran World Federation might best serve the churches in their ongoing concern for Christian-Jewish relations. In order to keep the consultation small, quotas were set up for each country and the National

Committees were asked to appoint representatives to the Consultation. Since this was intended primarily as a methodological consultation it was felt that it would not be appropriate to invite representatives of the Jewish community to meet with us at this time.

The Consultation carried on its work along two lines:

I. A study section, which included a theological paper and reports from Lutheran study groups, as well as a report on the work being done by the WCC office on the Church and the Jewish People.

II. A practical section in which the consultation divided into three groups to deal with specific recommendations to the Lutheran World Federation, member churches and their congregations, and study groups in the various countries.

I

The basic theological paper under the theme "Election and Justification in View of the Relation Between Church and Synagogue" was presented by Pastor Reinhard Dobbert. He pointed out that this theme stands at the heart of all Christian-Jewish relations and must serve as the framework within which all dialogue takes place. When the church has not taken this question seriously and has dealt with peripheral matters to the exclusion of a clear biblical witness to the meaning of election and justification for both parties in the dialogue, the result has been a distortion of biblical truth and, therefore, a poisoning of relationships. Closely connected with this is the "burning problem of sin-forgiveness".

If Lutheranism is to make a "decisive contribution" to "the further development of the Christian-Jewish dialogue", Pastor Dobbert said, "there must be within Lutheranism certain further studies, which must be concerned with the following questions:

a) What role does the teaching of justification play in the publications of the LWF and the WCC (not only in the area of the Church and the Jewish People)?

b) What distortions of this message are to be found, or where are successful attempts made to express this message in contemporary terms?

c) What sketches, emphases and distortions are there today in general within theology?

d) What is being said today in the Church and Synagogue on the subject of sin?

e) How is the matter of discontinuity being discussed today in the Synagogue? What role, for example, does the problem of atheism in Israel have?

f) Is the theme of justification (not the concept, but the real thing) even really known in Judaism? Is there, for example, theological thinking done concerning the justification for the political struggle of existence?"

The Rev. Johan Snoek of the WCC had been requested by staff to prepare a response to the Dobbert paper. Pastor Snoek pointed out that it is unrealistic to say that "Christendom must repeatedly attempt to speak with one voice." There is a plurality of voices among Jews as well as Christians. "Even within the different denominations there are deep divisions. We should not sweep differences under the carpet by trying to speak 'with one voice' but rather bring tensions out in the open and try to deal sensibly with them."

It was pointed out that the essayist himself had said that the Lutheran Church did not regard the "doctrine of election and justification of mankind in Christ Jesus" as the "proprium" of Lutheranism but as a "proprium of the Christian message". Rather than speak of a specific "Lutheran contribution" to the Jewish-Christian dialogue would it not be better to speak of a "special benefit" for Lutherans to be derived from the dialogue with the Jews? Lutherans might benefit greatly in such concepts as "two dominions", "law and Gospel" and "justification" through dialogue with Jews.

Pastor Snoek pointed out that if the essayist is correct in stating that the Church must be in "a constant discussion with the Synagogue, for without this vis-à-vis the church is in constant danger of misunderstanding its own nature", then "the special concerns of this consultation and of this paper should be exposed to the criticism of those who—though committed Christians—do not share this concern for Christian-Jewish dialogue."

The full text of Pastor Dobbert's paper and Pastor Snoek's response are available from Geneva on request.

Since May 1971 the WCC office has involved the churches in a study program on the subject of "Biblical Interpretation and its Bearing on Christian Attitudes Regarding the Situation in the Middle East". It was felt that such a study might serve "to avoid misuse of the Bible in support of partisan views". Christians are deeply divided in their evaluation of the situation in the Middle East. An analysis of their biblical assumptions may enable "the Church to be more effectively an instrument of reconciliation" since their "present divergencies paralyze the churches' efforts in this respect". It is one of the aims of the program to bring together people of divergent viewpoints so that differences can be faced honestly and openly and, even though such differences may not be resolved, possibilities for common action might be found.

Pastor Snoek pointed out that there is deep polarization in the church between those who support a "theology of the land" and see in recent historic events a fulfilment of Old Testament promises, and those who espouse a "theology of the poor" and, therefore, side with the Palestinian refugees.

Another important factor in the discussion is the difference of conceptions regarding the relationship of the Old and the New Testament. In order to help the study groups, a 17-point questionnaire was drawn up. Study groups have been established in Finland, Sweden, Norway, Denmark, Germany and France. Material was also received from Israel and the Lebanon. Many Lutheran groups participated in this study. A notable gap in the program was the absence of any study groups on this subject in North America.

Pastor Snoek also reported on the program of dialogue with Jewish leaders which is carried on by the World Council of Churches. In 1965 and 1968 informal meetings were held between representatives of the WCC and a number of Jewish leaders. An "International Jewish Committee on Interreligious Consultations" was set up. Since 1970 regular meetings of the two groups have been held. Apart from the discussion of religious themes, an important aspect of these meetings has been the discussion of general themes in which Christians and Jews have common interests as fellow members of the human community. Such themes as the problems of violence, racism in Southern Africa, human rights in the Soviet Union, the Middle East conflict, and the Bible and social justice, have established a climate of mutual and common concern which fosters good will and cooperation.

The participants in the Consultation expressed their interest in the work of the WCC and their deep appreciation of what is being done through that office on behalf of the Lutheran Churches as well. It was pointed out that some of the churches make only a minimal contribution to that work and some do not contribute at all. The Consultation felt that the WCC office was carrying out this program also on behalf of the Lutheran Churches and did much to further their concerns for the Jewish People. For this reason the Consultation resolved to recommend to the various National Committees that they allocate grants to the work which Pastor Snoek is doing in the World Council while at the same time continuing their support of the parallel and supplementary work done in the Lutheran World Federation.

II

The following recommendations given here are the text which was adopted by the Consultation as a whole.

A.   On the Work of The Church and the Jewish People in General
The members of this Consultation are convinced that the relation of the Church with the Jewish People is so important for the Christian self-understanding and for the whole Church, and the improvement of relationships so crucial, that studies and work in this area must be intensified. In this connection we recall that the Commission on Studies of the Lutheran World Federation has set the following guidelines for the

furtherance of studies on the Church and the Jewish People. The Commission on Studies sees its work in this field being done along three lines:

1.   The furtherance of study work in the member churches and between member churches. collaboration to be sought with other churches and specialized institutes;
2.   Cooperation with the World Council of Churches;
3.   Consultations or conferences for evaluation of the study work and the exploitation of basic theological and methodological questions.

B.   *On Structuring of Studies*
1.   We have discussed in detail the organizational form for studies in this area of concern: in the LWF Commission and Department of Studies; on the national level; through task forces; and on the local level.

It is *recommended* that further group work take place, if possible in the form of a new committee, in any event in task forces with specific assignments.

In this connection a new consultation along the lines described in Guidelines point 3 above should be planned for the near future.

2.   We are grateful for the work which the Commission on Studies of the LWF has previously accomplished in this area. We are convinced, however, that the expanding work outlined under 1 above can be successfully carried forward only if suitable staff assistance is provided. The members of this Consultation therefore *request* the LWF for provision for staff assistance for this area of concern. At the same time the request is made of the national committees (or similar organizations) to support this request as emphatically as possible (especially financial support). Several organizations represented at this Consultation have already indicated a willingness to help financially in this particular project.

The functions for this staff assignment would include:
furtherance and coordination of studies on various levels;
preparation for study groups and consultations;
evaluation and publication of study materials;
cooperation with the corresponding office in the World Council of
     Churches, as well as with national and local groups and institutes;
a central clearing house for literature and information.

C.   *On Methodology for Studies and Conversation*
Distinction must be made among intra-Lutheran discussion, inter-confessional dialogue, and conversations with Jews. For the themes (mentioned below) for study, the following points ought to be noted: In the present situation, what is important for Christian-Jewish conversation? (What is already included in the conversation? What should be included in the future?) What questions must Lutherans clarify further among themselves with reference to conversation with Jews?

D. On Themes for Study and Conversation

Among the major areas and themes the following are significant:

1. *Church and Synagogue*
   God-talk (how we speak of God);
   Election, Covenant, and People of God;
   Judaism as a living religion;
   The relation of the Old Testament and the New;
   Sin, guilt, and suffering;
   Jewish and Christian anthropology;
   Our common heritage.

   For us, further clarification of our understanding of justification, law, and especially Christology is necessary with regard to these above questions.

2. *Dialogue and Mission*
   Various ways and levels of encounter and conversation;
   Goal and aim (including the question of conversion, proselytism, and witness);
   Media (literature, etc.).

3. *The State of Israel*
   "Promise" (with reference to the land);
   Jewish and Arab minorities in the Middle East.

4. *Anti-Semitism*
   Luther and the Jews;
   Anti-Semitism in the New Testament;
   Anti-Semitism in modern literature, textbooks, worship materials, etc.

5. *General Themes*
   The search for World Community;
   Human rights;
   Peace and justice;
   Cooperation with communities of persons of other faiths;
   Problems of violence;
   Problems of racism.

The discussion of these general themes is suggested because it is hoped that Christian-Jewish conversation will not only deal with issues of direct interest to the Jewish and Christian communities but will also seek to serve the wider community of mankind.

E. On "Jerusalem"

In view of the concern of the Neuendettelsau Consultation on the Church and the Jewish People for the presence of the Lutheran Church in the Holy Land we submit the following.

Recommendations:

1. Information has reached this conference that at a recent synod meeting of the Evangelical Lutheran Church in Jordan it was decided to apply for

membership in the LWF. This Consultation rejoices in this decision and encourages the LWF Executive Committee to give serious consideration to this application for membership, recognizing how important it is that the Evangelical Lutheran Church in Jordan established active relationship with the worldwide Lutheran family.

2.   The Commission on Studies be asked to request the LWF Executive Committee to authorize an early consultation of representatives of the LWF Commissions as well·as local representatives from the Holy Land area and their supporting constituents for open discussion on such issues as follows:

a) The proposed Lutheran Centre in Jerusalem. (This Consultation felt that such a centre should not be a competing educational institute but should encourage cooperation with educational program facilities available in the area such as the Swedish Theological Institute, the Ecumenical Institute, the Hebrew University, etc.)

b) The future use of the Augusta Victoria Foundation Hospital.

c) The necessity of a Lutheran Representative in the area. The proposed consultation should assume responsibility to prepare a job description for this position.

There will be other issues that should be added to the agenda which we are not prepared to identify now (e.g. certain items in the report of the former LWF Committee on the Church and the Jewish People to the Fifth Assembly of LWF).

This Consultation recommends that, in preparation for the proposed "Jerusalem" consultation, talks should be initiated between representatives of the different Lutheran groups in Israel and representatives of the LWF.

3.   We note that some Christians in the Holy Land face anxieties and difficulties because of their faith. Where assistance and encouragement from the LWF might help people to remain to work out their Christian calling we suggest that this be provided. This will require some special research and study on the part of the LWF.

4.   The Commission on Studies be asked to encourage the General Secretariat of the LWF to seek to obtain "personal status" as a church for the Lutheran congregations in Israel.

5.   We have been advised by Rev. Terray that the Norwegian Israel Mission, in cooperation with other Lutheran agencies, plans to build an old peoples' home on LWF property in Haifa, presently housing worship facilities for the Lutheran Congregation there. We commend these cooperating Lutheran agencies for reaching out to meet this need. *We recommend* that the Board of Trustees of the LWF endorse this extended use of LWF property in Haifa.

F.   On Concerns on the Local Level

Certain aspects of Christian-Jewish relations are of primary importance for local congregations and national churches. These issues and activities must be pursued on the local level, with some assistance and direction given by national church offices and agencies. The problems and activities to which we call attention will vary in nature from one country to another, but we believe there are common elements which represent the interest of all participants in this Consultation.

1. We urge that Christian congregations should care for their Jewish neighbours and should seek to establish relationships with them. We see three levels of caring or relationship:

   a) On the level of our common humanity, Christian people should take the initiative in promoting friendly relationships with their Jewish neighbours. As fellow-citizens, Jews and Christians have common problems and obligations. Wherever possible and desirable Christians should make common cause with Jews in matters of civic and social concern. Mutual acquaintance and respect are essential to the well-being of both Christians and Jews.

   b) On the level of concern for minority groups, Christians should give all possible assistance to their Jewish neighbours in the struggle against prejudice, discrimination, and persecution. Without sharing a common creed, Jews and Christians may cooperate to the fullest extent in fostering human rights.

   c) On the level of religious commitment, Christians should invite Jews to engage in a mutual sharing of faith. Christians are not in a position to tell their Jewish neighbours that they should engage in such activities nor can they prescribe the manner in which this should be done. But Christian faith is marked by the impulse to bear witness to the grace of God in Jesus Christ. To bear such witness is intended as a positive, not a negative act. Witness, whether it be called 'mission' or 'dialogue', includes a desire both to know and to be known more fully. When we speak of a mutual sharing of faith we do not endorse syncretism. But we understand that when Christians and Jews speak to each other about matters of faith, there will be an exchange which calls for openness, honesty, love, and mutual respect. One cannot reveal his faith to another without recognizing the real differences that exist and being willing to take the risk of confronting these differences. We are using the words 'witness', 'mission', and 'dialogue', which have come to be labels for distinctive ways of sharing faith. These words have a different content for different Christians. We see problems in the use of these words and urge that Christian people give attention to exploring their meanings.

   Although these relationships must be established on the local level, with assistance from national offices and agencies, we *recommend* that the LWF promote these activities by facilitating the exchange of information and materials on the international level.

2. In the light of the increasing number of interfaith marriages in several countries, we believe that new dimensions and approaches in pastoral counseling are urgent. Such interfaith marriages may lead to the conversion of one partner or the other, or they may lead to the breaking of connections with both synagogue and church, or they may become cells for on-going Christian-Jewish dialogue. We do not urge that interfaith marriages be seen as another means of promoting conversions to the Christian faith. But we do wish to urge that the churches should be aware of the increasing need for a special kind of pastoral help for the sake of strengthening the unity of families and the faith of individuals. This need should be met by new techniques in the training of pastors.

We urge that the LWF transmit this concern to the appropriate agencies.

3. We urge that the churches have an important educational task to perform in the area of Jewish-Christian relations.

a) We reaffirm the message of the Logumkloster Declaration with respect to the importance of continuing the struggle against anti-Semitism in any form. We note with approval that during recent years several member churches of the LWF have made substantial progress in the effort to remove from Christian publications false and misleading statements about Jews. These efforts have often been made in consultation with Jewish scholars. We must continue to oppose the 'teaching of contempt' wherever it may be found.

We urge that churches should produce and offer suitable materials for religious education both in church schools and, wherever possible, in public schools. It is also necessary that churches should design programs of instruction aimed at changing the attitudes of teachers who use these materials.

We *recommend* that the LWF transmit this concern to member churches.

b) We recognize the phenomenon of tourism today, especially the increase of travel to the Holy Land. Many of these tours are advertised as 'Lutheran' enterprises. We believe that such travel and exposure can have both positive and negative results with respect to inter-group relationships and inter-faith understanding. For the benefit of such tourists and their leaders we encourage Lutheran publishing houses to give special attention to the preparation of informative materials which will provide an accurate, balanced, and reconciling picture of the situation in the Middle East today. We recognize that some churches have already produced useful publications. We recommend that agencies of the national churches take further initiatives in the preparation of such materials and find ways of making them available to tourists and travel agencies. Such action would do much to prevent misunderstanding and to increase the positive results of travel. We *recommend* that the LWF serve as the channel for the international exchange of such materials.

The Oneness of God and the Uniqueness of Christ: Christian Witness and the Jewish People. Report of a Consultation held under the auspices of the Lutheran World Federation. Oslo, Norway, 1975.

A. The Oneness of God
When we as Christians speak about God we refer to the God to whom Holy Scripture bears witness. He revealed Himself to His chosen people of Isreal, and we are indebted to them for this witness. The conviction that God is one, claiming exclusive allegiance, matured in them from the beginning and they held to it through many periods of danger and suffering. In this, Israel was always different from the other nations, who acknowledged and worshipped a number of gods.

Together with the Jews, we confess the one God. The fundamental Jewish confession of faith the Shema Yisrael ("Hear, O Israel, the Lord our God is one Lord", Deut 6:4), is the obvious background of the Christian creed. We also share the Jews' faith in God's creative power over the whole world and in His will to save all mankind as attested in the Old Testament.

B. The Uniqueness of Christ
Christians make these statements only in conjunction with the affirmation that for them faith in the one god is indissolubly linked with confessing the uniqueness of Jesus Christ. Thus they witness to and call upon the one God as the Father of Jesus Christ.

The conviction of the first Christians that the final realization of the Kingdom of God had begun in Jesus Christ was grounded in and strengthened by encounter with the risen Christ. That the crucified one is the Messiah through whom came salvation and redemption has always remained basic to the Christian faith and was exuberantly expressed in the statement of the early church: "And there is salvation in no one else, for there is no other name under heaven given among men by which we must be saved" (Acts 4:12).

In this conviction, Christians began to discover and read the Scriptures in a new way. A variety of Old Testament affirmations on the way of salvation were brought into focus and related directly to Jesus in the attempt to describe the experience of his uniqueness. They thereby confessed Jesus as the way to the Father for all mankind, both Jews and Gentiles.

C. Judaism and Christianity: A Mutual Challenge
This statement of faith marked the parting of the ways for Jews and Christians. However, a relationship between Judaism and the church still

remains. The fact that both move forward from the same Old Testament starting-point is a constant reciprocal challenge for Christians and Jews.

Paul was concerned with the special relationship between Christians and Jews in his Letter to the Romans. Chapters 9-11 bear witness to his grappling with this question. He emphasizes that God has not disowned His people. He warns the Gentile Christians against arrogance vis-à-vis the Jews, and expects a final gathering of all those who belong to God.

In the post-biblical age the Christian doctrine of the true God and the true humanity and divinity of Christ was developed on the basis of the rich store of New Testament statements about the uniqueness of Jesus Christ. This doctrine is meant to express and preserve faith in the one God in light of the overwhelming experience of the uniqueness of Jesus Christ and the power of the Holy Spirit. Hence the Nicene Creed opens with the words, "We believe in one God . . ."

But this doctrine has not always protected us against misunderstandings. For example, the experience of the uniqueness of Jesus Christ and the concentration of all statements of faith on him have not infrequently resulted in giving all attention to Jesus, thus tending to eclipse God. His will to be the way to the Father is thereby obscured, as is also his will to return his kingdom to the Father at the end (\Cor 15:24-28).

The existence of Judaism poses a continuing question as to whether we as Christians keep our faith in the one God. Christian-Jewish conversation can help to avoid imprecise speech about God. This is important for all Christian language about Him.

When Jews concern themselves with Jesus, he is seen as a man. This can help us as Christians to take Jesus' humanity completely seriously. In Judaism particular importance is attached to the obedience which is realized in just actions. Judaism thus reminds Christianity that the one God wants our witness to Him not only in word, but also in deed.

D. Christian Witness

1. The Nature of Christian Witness

Christians need to remember that their witness to the Jewish people is but part and parcel of their witness to all people. There has sometimes been the misperception that Jews are to be isolated in a class by themselves, and then either singled out for exclusive missionary attention or excluded from Christian mission altogether. But this would assume that Jews are qualitatively different from ourselves, and furthermore that it is something about ourselves - perhaps that we are the have's and others are the have-not's - that generates Christian witness. That would be to forget that Christian witness, whether to Judaism or to anyone else, is God's mission and not our own. Christians, no less than others, are sinners and share in the common crisis of all mankind under divine judgement. "We are beggars," said Luther, and all we have is pure gift.

Christians have always been witnessing to their faith. "As the Father sent me, so I send you" (Jn 22:21). But that very sending reminds us that salvation in Christ is an action of God embracing all mankind. It is God who saves the world. The Christians through their witness only share the benefits of this salvation and the good news about it. They know that in Christ Jesus God has already deeded these gifts to all mankind, and not only to those who happen already to be enjoying them.

2. Christian Witness and the Jewish People

The Christian witness is directed toward all our fellowmen, including the Jewish people. In witnessing to Jews, however, we must be mindful of the unique historical and spiritual relationship we have with them, both in continuity and discontinuity.

Among Jewish people, no Christian witness would suffice which does not gratefully affirm and live out what they and we have in common. Yet it is that very continuity between us which intensifies the discontinuity. To minimize this unique discontinuity, therefore, would likewise be evasive and artificial. The coming of Christ and the challenge of his gospel place Judaism in a situation of crisis. No Christian witness can be unsympathetic with that, seeing how Christians themselves face a similar crisis before the same Christ. Having done so as Christians, however, they cannot abandon the New Testament proclamation even though they must recognize that that proclamation continues to put contemporary Judaism under the same original challenge. Yet there is only one way for Christian witness to share in that ordeal, namely, in the same compassion and solidarity with the hearers that Christ has displayed towards Christians themselves, and with the same concern he has for every aspect of the hearer's entire well-being.

E. Jewish-Christian Relations: Repentance and Hope

This topic has been studied carefully in the past and has been described in several documents previously issued by the LWF, its member churches, and other Christian bodies. In what follows we intend to offer some suggestions which will serve as addenda to these statements.

When we speak of the guilt and responsibility of Lutherans and other Christians in having fostered and allowed anti-Semitism, we should not give the impression that Christianity is simply identified with the old "Western" (and "Eastern") churches. The arrogant habit of describing Western experience as if it were global must be discontinued. The churches of Asia and Africa have not had the same part in this sordid history. We urge them, however, to define and expose the potential or actual forms of anti-Semitism that may be theirs.

We Lutherans must be aware of our peculiar forms of potential and actual anti-Semitism. An undiscriminating disparagement of the Law in our theology, preaching, instruction, and piety frequently has as its tragic result a caricaturing of the Jew as the epitome of hypocrisy and self-righteousness to the point of putting the label of "Judaizing" upon the common human tendency towards legalism. This fact emphasizes the need to study this problem and to invite Jewish scholars to examine our materials for this kind of anti-Semitism.

Jesus said: "If you are offering your gift at the altar, and there remember that your brother has something against you . . ." (Mt 5:23). Not least in Jewish-Christian relations is this word an important one. For here the question is not only about *our* feelings of love and *our* rights to witness, but also of whether others have something against us. That is why we must listen to the Jewish community. We must sense their pain and hear their voice on the question of the threat and reality of anti-Semitism and of how to improve Jewish-Christian relations. Christian documents are by now rich in admissions of guilt for past sins. Some of our Jewish friends will tell us that our guilt feelings do them little good. They may benefit us even less. Our repentance is worthy of the name only if it leads to change, to renewed hope, to prayer and work for a better future. An essential step is to ask our Jewish neighbours what hurts them. A rabbinic story tells of the excited student who said to his teacher, "Rabbi, I love you." The rabbi replied, "Do you know what hurts me?" The student answered, "No." The rabbi asked, "How then can you say that you love me?"

The conflict in the Middle East raises difficult questions about the future of the Jewish people, the rights of Palestinian Arabs and the problems of all refugees. Lutherans and other Christians are painfully aware of the fact that Christianity has for 19 centuries been a source of anti-Semitic thought and action. We cannot confess our guilty involvement in the Holocaust of the 1940s without committing ourselves to action that will prevent the repetition of such a tragedy. We must say, "Never Again!" We know that the right to live cannot be securely enjoyed unless peace is achieved. We therefore call upon Lutheran churches to make responsible contributions toward the achievement of peace and reconciliation, justice and dignity, among all the peoples of the Middle East.

F. Prospectus for the Future

It has been the practice of Lutherans to approach their responsibilities by giving careful attention to the biblical and theological aspects of problems. The topic of Lutheran-Jewish relationships for example has been studied over a long period of time by individual scholars, and during the past decade several significant statements have been issued by Lutheran churches in various countries and by Lutheran World Federation conferences. These statements do not constitute a final or complete treatment of the topic, but they have spoken to the important questions and indicate a growing concern among Lutherans.

At this point, it is easy to see that further study should be given to many topics. Some of these topics need to be clarified among Lutherans and others should be discussed with representatives of the Jewish community. We have in mind such themes as election, covenant, and the people of God; Judaism as a living religion; the relation of the Old Testament and the New; the significance of the law; sin, guilt, and suffering; Jewish and Christian anthropology; the goals, aims, and procedures of mission and dialogue; the historical and present dimensions and remedies of anti-Semitism; the theological and moral implications of the Holocaust; the meaning of Judaism for Christian self-understanding; the significance of the State of Israel in its Middle Eastern context; and the search for peace, justice, and human rights throughout the human community.

Such topics will always need further study and will no doubt continue to be examined by individuals and groups. Emphasis should now be placed upon the *dissemination* and *use* of studies and declarations that are our common possession. In the pursuit of this objective, European and American committees are now able to give more effective leadership in the collection, interpretation, and distribution of useful study documents.

Unless Lutheran position papers have some practical consequence on regional and local levels, the studies will have been made in vain. We believe that the process of study, publication, and interaction with other Lutherans and Jews should continue regionally and locally. But we also believe that the Lutheran World Federation can perform essential services for its member churches as all Lutherans work together to deepen their sense of solidarity with the sufferings of the Jewish people. We therefore urge the Lutheran World Federation, through its appropriate offices, to:

1. Maintain contact between groups in several continents which are conducting studies and formulating policies with respect to Lutheran-Jewish relations. Commissions have already been formed in Europe and America which have the function of furthering the exchange of studies and information, and promoting engagement in common projects. This work is being carried out in the form of working parties, study conferences, and publications. These commissions will coordinate these tasks within the churches so far as it is desirable and possible.

2. Cooperate in all possible ways with the World Council of Churches' Committee on the Church and the Jewish People and with other ecumenical agencies, such as the Vatican's Commission for Religious Relations with the Jews, in the pursuit of objectives mentioned above. Cooperation should also occur at the local level between congregations and between inter-church agencies.

3. Collect materials that have to do with Lutheran-Jewish relations, and serve as a channel for their distribution. Work has already been done on the development of materials for ministers and congregations. Information has been prepared, for example, which will help pastors approach such texts as those which have been assigned for the 10th Sunday after Trinity (i.e., dealing with the destruction of Jerusalem). Close cooperation in this activity with the Lutheran World Federation and through the Lutheran World Federation with other churches is of highest importance. The Lutheran World Federation can serve as a clearing house of information about activities in member churches, studies conducted by theological faculties, educational materials, etc. We urge that theological faculties be regularly informed about such studies. It is important that Lutherans share with each other what they know about developments in this field of interest.

4. Encourage and facilitate the production of good educational materials for practical use on the regional and local levels. We urge the Lutheran World Federation staff to develop a strategy for making contact with educational commissions and publishing houses of the churches.

5. Remind all Lutheran agencies of the importance of consulting with representatives of the Jewish community when statements about Lutheran-Jewish relations are being prepared. Some churches have made, and continue to make, analyses of their literature with reference to explicit or implicit anti-Semitism. We urge those of our member churches that have not done so to begin this task immediately and that, if at all possible, Jews be drawn in as consultants. We also recommend that when Jews are invited to attend conferences as consultants, they be included in the planning stage.

6. Hold occasional conferences for the purpose of facilitating new initiatives in study and action, to give a more adequate expression of a common mind among Lutherans, and to induct new persons into the field of study and work.

7. Take steps to prevent the isolation of Lutheran-Jewish relations from the area of mission in general. We propose that Lutheran-Jewish acivities be pursued in concert with the Lutheran World Federation Department of Church Cooperation.

8. Provide suitable staff support for the international coordination of Lutheran efforts to approach Jews in a responsible manner. We are aware of financial problems, but we give such high priority to this work that we urge the establishment of a separate desk or office in the Lutheran World Federation to deal with Lutheran-Jewish relations. We also recommend that a small advisory group be established to work with the Department of Studies staff both in following up the recommendations of this consultation and in planning for additional work in the area of Lutheran-Jewish concerns.

9. Recommend to member churches that in each country or church, where feasible, a central office or desk be established for responsibilities for Lutheran-Jewish concerns similar to those carried by the Lutheran World Federation.

10. Give place to Lutheran-Jewish concerns both in the planning and on the agenda of the 1977 Lutheran World Federation Assembly.

Christians and Jews. A Study by the Council of the Evangelical Church in Germany. 1975. (By kind permission of Guetersloher Verlagshaus Gerd Mohn, translated from the German.)

I. Common Roots

1. One God

When we Christians speak of God, we are of one mind with the Jews that the God to whom the Holy Scriptures bear witness, is One. Since the early period of Israel, it has been a fundamental principle that God as Creator and Redeemer lays claim to exclusiveness. It was in this that the Jews of the Old Testament era differed from other nations who recognized and worshipped several or even many gods. Witness to the One God was also a mark of Christians, and during the first centuries of Christian history Jews and Christians were equally maligned and persecuted for it.

The basic Jewish *credo* in our time as in those days, is: "Hear, o Israel, the Lord is our God, the Lord is One" (Dt 6:4). Jesus and His disciples also pronounced these words as part of their daily prayers, as the Jews do even today. That same statement became the basis of the first article of the Christian confession of faith.

The link is also evident in the development of this confession by Jews and Christians. Faith in God the Creator is placed at the beginning of the Bible; it has pervaded Jewish prayer from its beginning and is a central article of Christian faith. Jews and Christians understand God as the God of all mankind while, at the same time, He has a particular relationship with those who belong to His people.

This relationship finds particular expression in man's faith in God, the Redeemer. The Old Testament attests to the experience of this faith in various ways: from the miraculous delivery of the people of Israel from Egyptian bondage to the expectation of the final return and redemption of the entire people. That theme was taken up by the New Testament and marked by a new experience: faith in the divine acts of Jesus' death and resurrection, the support of the Holy Spirit in the period between Easter and the Second Coming of Christ, and the expectation of redemption at the end of time. Hope in the resurrection of the dead, alluded to in the Old Testament, was further developed by Judaism at the time of Jesus. Since then, it has been an essential element of Jewish prayer language while in Christian expectations of the end of time, it is indissolubly joined to belief in the Resurrection of Jesus Christ.

Quite often elements characteristic of and basic to, Christianity are also distinctive of Jewish piety. In Jewish prayers which for many centuries have been passed on from generation to generation, God the Creator and Redeemer who raises the dead, is addressed and praised as the merciful and compassionate one and Father of His own. Love for His people and for all men and assurance of the forgiveness of our sins is expressed in a variety of ways.

In Christian faith, these statements stand in the context of God's revelation in Christ. This is most clearly expressed in the One God who is confessed and invoked as the Father of Jesus Christ.

2. Holy Scripture

The first Christians, like all Jews, had a number of biblical books which basically corresponded to what the Church later called the "Old Testament". These writings are in the New Testament called, "the Law and the Prophets" (Mt 22:40). Frequently they are simply called the Scriptures since this collection was generally known and recognized as a fundamental testimony of faith. Christians as well as Jews derived abundant instruction from the Scriptures for everyday life, prayer, sermons, and worship.

In proclaiming His message, Jesus quite naturally referred to the Scriptures as they were available to Him. The dual command of love which He made the nucleus of His message, was derived from the Scriptures by connecting two originally separate statements: "You shall love the Lord your God with all your heart, and with all your soul, and with all your strength" (Dt 6:5) and, "You shall love your neighbor as yourself" (Lv 19:18). This was a permissible procedure within the framework of Jewish Scriptural interpretation of the time. Thus the learned Jew talking to Jesus agreed, "well answered, Master" (Mk 12:32). By applying this command to enemies, tax collectors, and Samaritans, Jesus drew consequences from it, though, that went beyond Jewish interpretations.

Following Jesus, Paul made the Scriptures the basis for his proclamation and employed the rules common to Jewish interpretation at his time. It is noteworthy that Paul refers to words of Jesus in a few passages only while quoting the Scriptures very frequently. Yet, he also interprets the latter in a new way that is strange to Jews.

These Scriptures are common to Jews and Christians. They are made known to non-Jews in the Christian proclamation. Paul already addressed himself to Gentiles and from that time on, non-Jews became familiar with the relationship of God with His people Israel and were taken into that history.

The Christian communities' own writings begin at an early stage. They refer constantly to the "Scriptures" while developing God's saving acts in Jesus Christ. These form the "New Testament" which Christians joined to the "Old Testament" to form their Bible.

Again and again in the course of her history, the Church has struggled to comprehend the Old Testament. There also were repeated attempts to deprive individual books of their worth or deny recognition to the Old Testament as a whole, as part of Holy Scripture. Such attempts were rejected by the Church, however, because she confesses the God of Abraham, Isaac, and Jacob as Father of Jesus Christ. Thus, the Old

Testament, the Holy Scripture of the Jews, remains one of the two components of the Christian Bible.

3. The People of God

According to Old Testament belief, God is the Creator and Lord of the world as well as the God of His people Israel whom He chose and with whom He made a covenant. That is due, not to the virtues or merits of His people, but to a bestowal of the love of God.

Love of God for His people demands the people's love for their God which finds expression in doing His will. Israel, as a people, is to live according to the commandments revealed at Sinai. Even though the people as a whole may be found wanting in the required obedience, the Prophets proclaim that God holds to His election and calls His people to repentance so that they may completely fulfill His will.

This basic self-understanding as people of God is a determinant of Jews even of our day. This finds frequent expression in prayer where it says: "Thou hast chosen us and hast hallowed us among the nations." Though it is known that a large proportion of the people do not completely fulfill the commandments of God, Jewish tradition says: "All of Israel have a share in the coming world." The divine election remains valid for the sake of the covenant which God made with the fathers.

The New Testament, too, speaks of the people of God which, initially, refers to the people of Israel. Jesus says that He is sent to "the lost sheep of the house of Israel" (Mt 15:24). And Paul confirms to the Jews that they are and will remain the people of God: "God has not rejected His people" (Rom 11:2). He expects them to be included—either now or in the future—in the salvation revealed by Christ.

The barriers of belonging to a particular people are abolished in the Christian proclamation of the Gospels; all who believe in Jesus Christ are children of Abraham and heirs to the promise given to Israel. This is how the Church, the people of God from among the Jews and Gentiles, was born.

Together with the concept "people of God", the New Testament transfers basic elements of Old Testament covenantal thinking to the Christian community. The latter are called, "a chosen race, a royal priesthood, a holy nation, God's own people" (1 Pet 2:9), just as the Old Testament says of the people of Israel (Ex 19:5-6).

Thus, Jews and Christians understand themselves as people of God. Despite their division, both are called and ordained to be witnesses of God in this world, to do His will, and to move toward the future fulfillment of His reign.

4. Worship

Jews and Christians gather for worship to hear the word of God, to confess their faith, and to pray. There. are common elements in their worship which distinguish them from most other religions. These are based on the fact that both consider themselves bound by divine revelation to which the Holy Scriptures bear witness. Both cover all of the life of a devout person who, in faith and obedience to the word of God, should make all his life an expression of worship.

The present forms of Jewish worship are the result of a long development. In the course of this process, the Temple worship in Jerusalem with its offerings existed side by side with prayer services in synagogues, which could be held anywhere. After the destruction of the Temple in 70 AD, the synagogue service became the core of Jewish religious life. Christian worship, which had its origin in the celebration of the Lord's Supper, took over elements of the synagogue service and developed them independently.

Jewish and Christian worship, then, contain many similarities and hold many things in common, e.g. the weekly holiday (Sabbath/Sunday), the form of the word service (Scripture readings, prayers, blessings) with common liturgical expressions (Alleluyah, Amen), certain celebrations in the course of the year (Passover/Easter) and in the course of life (circumcision/baptism, affirmation of the hope for a future life at the burial of the dead). We must not overlook that existing differences were often created with the intent to separate one from the other.

Similarities in structure and form of the liturgical services permitted the first Christians to maintain their community with Jews by taking part in synagogue services. After a long period of separate development, reflections on the fellowship of Christians and Jews have led to attempts to worship together again, on certain occasions.

5. *Justice and Love*
Christians and Jews are characterized in their self-understanding by the knowledge that they were chosen by God as partners to His covenant. In that election God reveals His love and His justice, from which grows the obligation for Jews and Christians alike, to work for a realization of justice and love in the world.

In all that God does, justice and love are one; that is why they should be one in man. Human justice must at all time be inspired by love, while human love depends on justice. Whether or not they are fulfilling this claim, greatly influences the credibility of Christians and Jews.

The Old Testament applies the commandment of love primarily to the people of God as partner in the Covenant. But it is also said of the stranger who lives with the people: "You shall love him as yourself" (Lv 19:34).

Certain groups in post-biblical Judaism extended the commandment for love of neighbor still further, while Jesus did away with all limitations by calling for love of the enemy.

The requirement for a life in justice, determined in all its particulars by obedience to the will of God, is strongly emphasized in Judaism. That could create the impression as if love were supplanted by justice. Yet, the Old Testament prophets as well as later teachers of Judaism justified such a life by the love of God for His people: Out of love, God gave the Torah to His people. It comprises that sphere of life in which righteousness is realized in love of neighbor, as a response to that act of God.

In Christian understanding, too, justice and love belong together; but Christians consider God's act of justification in Jesus Christ a prerequisite to the realization of justice and love among men.

Thus, profound differences exist between Christians and Jews for the justification of love and justice; yet they hold much in common in the perception of concrete demands. For that reason, Christians and Jews can cooperate in the realization of justice and love in the world and in the service of peace.

6. *History and Fulfillment*

In their relationship to history and its final goal, Jews and Christians are bound together by the experiences of the people of Israel in their history with God, ever since the time of Abraham.

Among the nations of that time, it was widely held that mankind and the world were at the mercy of fate in an eternal cycle of birth and death. The people of Israel, however, knew by experience—though often against their own ideas and wishes—that God was calling them on a way that knows no return. This road is leading toward a goal where Israel, together with the other nations, will receive final salvation in God.

Under the influence of such experiences, Jews and Christians believe that the process of history must not be seen as blind fate or a chain of erratic events. They realize and bear witness to the fact that the ultimate meaning and goal of history is God's salvation for all men.

Christians believe that in Jesus Christ the prophecies of God's covenant with His people have gained a new and wider dimension to bring the world closer to fulfillment. It is at this point that we find the strain underlying the division: For Jews it is the Torah that leads to fulfillment, while for Christians salvation lies in faith in the Messiah Jesus who has come already, and in the expectation of His second coming.

Despite this, the many things held in common by Christians and Jews obligate them to endure that tension and to make it fruitful for the fulfillment of history, expected by both. Christians and Jews are called to carry out their responsibilities for the world, not against or independent of one another, but jointly under the will of God.

II. *The Parting of the Ways*

1. *Belief in Jesus, the Christ*

Jews at the time of Jesus conceived of themselves as the one people of the One God. Within that people there existed various factions which often were at odds with each other. Hope and actions of most of these groups were directed toward the realization of salvation as promised by the prophets. In the face of an oppressing external situation, some of them expected the end of the present world and the coming of a new; others hoped for salvation in the unfolding of the reign of God which would include political freedom for the chosen people and the Holy Land, from the pagan Roman power. Long before Jesus' time, expectation of the Messiah, a saviour sent by God, played an important part.

Similar to John the Baptist, Jesus of Nazareth proclaimed: "The kingdom of God has come" (Mk 1:15; cf. Mt 3:2; 4:17). His proclamation of the Gospel and His mighty deeds aroused the expectation among those gathered about Him that He would save Israel. Thus a new group, centred around Jesus, came into being within the Jewish people, an event which in the beginning did not appear unusual.

Controversies soon became evident because Jesus gave unwonted interpretations to the religious traditions of His people on the impending reign of God and because He devoted Himself to the outcasts and sinners. The religious and political representatives in Jerusalem were offended by Jesus' manner and that of His followers and considered Him dangerous. Interaction between the Jewish autonomous administration and the Roman occupying power—so difficult to disentangle historically—finally led to the execution of Jesus by the Romans.

In the face of such a death, Jesus' disciples asked themselves whether or not their bond with Him as the Messiah had been proved erroneous. The reign of God had not come about in the expected manner and death by crucifixion was not only deeply humiliating but considered a refutation by God Himself, of their expectations of Jesus.

Their encounters with the Risen One reestablished and deepened the disciples' convictions that Jesus was the Messiah, the Christ; that deliverance and salvation were bound up with Him; that whoever trusts and believes in Him will be saved.

With this assurance, they began to proclaim that with the life, suffering, death, and resurrection of Jesus the time of salvation had come; in Him they saw the proof of the love of God for all men. The early Christian community perceived this event as the realization of the promises given to Israel and the nations. For that reason, they felt compelled to bear witness toward Jews and Gentiles, of their faith, hope, and love.

With this message, the first Christians meant to convince the other Jews of the truth of the claim that in Jesus the crucified and risen One the expected Messiah had come. They had to deal in this with other hopes of salvation and Messianic expectations which did not focus upon the person of Jesus as redeemer. Though they did not yet withdraw from the Jewish community, it was the beginning of the parting of the ways.

2. Interpretation of the Holy Scriptures

Jesus had set the inception of the promised reign of God and the double command of love as criteria for the understanding of Holy Scripture. His followers, furthermore, rediscovered the Bible in the light of their faith in the crucified and risen Jesus. They began to read the Scriptures as prophecy of Jesus Christ, His history, and His significance, as well as a witness to the preparation of salvation which in Him was fulfilled. This new conception of the Scriptures found expression in the gradually evolving writings which were later on combined in the "New Testament" and joined to the "Old Testament" to form a whole.

New Testament writings expressed the uniqueness of Jesus Christ in concepts borrowed from the Old Testament and the non-Jewish environment, thereby giving these terms eventually a new meaning. Among them were many sovereign titles, such as "Son of Man", "Messiah", "Son of God", "Lord", "Saviour", as well as expectations of salvation, such as the redemption of the world and the second coming of Jesus at the end of time. From the Jewish point of view, some of these statements appeared as a threat to the faith in the One God because Jesus was thereby made too much an equal of God. That referred mainly to statements in the Christian proclamation addressed to pagan hearers (cf. II, 4).

St. Paul's scriptural interpretations became particularly significant for succeeding Christian generations. Referring to the distinction between promise and law for a Christian understanding of the Old Testament, he maintains that the promises are fulfilled in Jesus Christ and the law has no further salvific meaning for Christians. This does not preclude but rather includes that a realization of the law in love is an imperative for the faithful.

In contradistinction to these interpretations relating to Christ, Judaism continued to develop its own ways of exegesis. After a period of oral tradition, scholarly interpretation of the Torah was recorded in various collections, in particular the Mishna and Talmud.

These divergent scriptural interpretations—Christians referring themselves to the person of Jesus Christ, Jews to the Torah—led to an ever increasing estrangement between Christians and Jews.

3. The Christian Community and the People of God

The first Christian communities were initially considered one of several credal groups within Judaism. Descriptions in the Acts of the Apostles and particularly the influence of St. Paul indicate developments, however, that soon went beyond the confines of the Jewish community. The Christian communities accepted not only Jews but an ever increasing number of Gentiles, without insisting that the latter become Jews. The percentage of Jewish Christians thereby continued to decrease.

As the Christian communities began to consist predominantly of non-Jewish members, they could no longer be acknowledged by Jews as a part of their people. Those Jews, therefore, who had been baptized in the name of Jesus, found it difficult to maintain fellowship with their people. Christians of different backgrounds were not much interested in such a fellowship, anyway.

The Christian community thus developed more and more into an independent entity. Admission to the community by baptism was considered an admission to the people of God, while the significance of membership by birth receded into the background. This is how the "Church of Jews and Gentiles" came into being.

The result was that Christians and Jews gave different meaning to the term "people of God". In the Jewish sense, it continued to mean belonging to the Jewish people. Thus, Jews as well as Christians claimed to be heirs to the history of the people of God since the days of Abraham. Christians, however, also ascribed certain ideas relating to Jesus Christ to the fellowship of the faithful. In doing so, they used the biblical concept of the people of God to describe themselves as "Church".

The conflict over membership in the people of God gravely tainted the relations between Christians and Jews, throughout the centuries. Right up to our time, there exists the problem whether one group's claim to be the people of God negates that of the other.

4. *The Developing Characteristics of Judaism and Christianity*

The relations between Jews and Christians became increasingly difficult because their understanding of piety developed along different lines.

A trend to emphasize obedience to the commandments of God became ever more prominent in Jewish daily life. Discourse on the application of the commandments and their influence on the most minute details of life was conducted with utmost diligence in the Jewish academies. Each generation considered the questions and answers of earlier ones and carried them further. Mishna and Talmud, collections of such conversations recorded over the centuries, serve as the basis for the religious life of the pious Jews even to our day.

Little emphasis was placed, however, on the definition and formulation of concepts of faith, which were transmitted in the narrative tradition, while prayers for public and private worship, as they were handed down over the centuries, form a particularly important element in the expression of Jewish piety.

In the Christian context, the necessity to develop the message of Jesus Christ and defend it against Greek ideas led to an intensive effort to clarify statements of faith and formulate an official doctrine of the Church.

An important problem was the description of the unique significance of Jesus Christ in the Christian faith and His relationship to the One and Only God. In the course of intensive theological efforts which were accompanied by severe struggles of church politics, the ancient Church replied to this question with the doctrine of the Triune God (the One God is acknowledged and worshipped in three "Persons"—Father, Son, and Holy Spirit) and that of the two Natures of Christ (Jesus Christ is "true God and true Man"). That teaching was based on New Testament statements and developed in the newly acquired forms of thinking.

To the Jewish mind, such doctrines were more and more an offense against the commandment that none but God must be worshipped as divine, while the Church, in these doctrines, continued to believe in the One God.

5. The Demarcation of Christianity from Judaism

The Jewish wars against Rome (66-70 and 132-135 AD) more or less put an end to the multiplicity of Jewish religious groups, leading toward stronger interior unity among Jews who had been widely scattered and robbed of their national sovereignty. In this context, a solemn condemnation of Jewish sects and Nazarenes (=Jewish Christians) became part of the "Prayer of Eighteen Petitions"—one of the most important Jewish prayers. At this point, a rupture with the Church took place. It had become practically impossible for Christians to take part in the Jewish liturgy. Before this, it had been quite usual for Jewish Christians to come to the synagogue while also attending Christian services, in particular, the celebration of the Eucharist.

Later passages in Jewish writings which consider Jesus the seducer of the Jewish people, presuppose an already accomplished break with the Church. They are not meant to add new information about the events around Jesus but to be a determined defense against the belief that Jesus is the Christ.

The Christian claim, as if the Church as the people of the Messiah was also heir to the covenant that God had made with Israel, provoked very severe judgments about the Jews in New Testament times. Such views could be based on certain words of Jesus about His people where He referred to the announced judgment day by Old Testament prophets. Later on, that event led to the assertion that God had rejected the people who opposed the Messiah Jesus. The destruction of Jerusalem in 70 AD as well as the fate of the Jewish people since that time were often interpreted as a confirmation of that opinion.

Yet, there also existed different interpretations; the Apostle Paul, in particular, wrestled with this problem. In chapters 9-11 of the Letter to the Romans, he deals with the prophetic condemnation of the people Israel but he also emphasizes that God has not rejected His people. Paul expects a unification of the whole people of God, at the end of time.

Discussions on prophetic criticism in Paul's writings and other New Testament books were held within the framework of the Jewish community. When non-Jews joined the Christian groups, however, the character of such statements was changed completely: they no longer were words by Jews about Jews but condemnations of the Jewish people by outsiders. That situation often led to self-righteous confidence within the Church vis à vis the Jews. In the end, the latter were considered aliens to such an extent that they were slandered as "murderers of God". Enmity against Jews often brought about, particularly since Christianity became a state religion, the use of violence against Jews, even murder of individuals and expulsion or destruction of whole Jewish communities and populations.

The relationship of Jews and Christians, right up to our time, is burdened by this past. Though acts of violence have largely ceased, many Christians still think of Jews as aliens, even enemies: enemies of Christ, hence of Christians.

Yet the relations between Jews and Christians were not exclusively characterized by animosity and violence. In the course of centuries, Judaism and Christianity exchanged ideas and influenced each other. Scriptural exegesis of the Reformation era, for instance, was greatly stimulated by Jewish exegetical tradition. At all times, there were conversions, not only from Judaism to Christianity but vice versa. Disputes between Christians and Jews obscured common ideas, yet that which united them was never completely lost.

III.   Jews and Christians Today

1.   The various Forms of Judaism and Christianity

Judaism as we know it today, is not uniform. Just as in former times, it bears the imprint of environmental intellectual trends. In the confrontation between Jewish tradition and European Enlightenment during the 19th and 20th centuries, varying views were developed. Some Jewish communities held fast to the traditional religious interpretation and form of synagogue services. Such *orthodox* Jews are concerned with the exact observation of the Torah, which to them is not a burden but joy. Ethical and cultic commandments are given equal emphasis. Scripture is accepted as directly inspired by God, which precludes scholarly Bible critique. The Talmud, too, is considered of binding authority.

Liberal *Reform* Judaism stands at the opposite end. Though not intending to change the contents of faith, it holds that form and interpretation should be developed; laws, customs, and institutions are adapted to changed situations. In synagogue services, for instance, Hebrew is used as well as the vernacular; ethical commandments are rated higher than e.g. food, fasting, cleanliness laws. Ethics and social justice are strongly emphasized.

Conservative Judaism stands between the two other groups. It holds more closely to old rituals and contents than Reform Judaism but admits historical change of religious customs and tradition. Since the Enlightenment, some Jews no longer conceive of Judaism as a religion, a view that was reinforced for many by the experience of Auschwitz.

In recent times, more emphasis has been placed on that which is common to all Jews. Despite differences and contradictions, they consider themselves more and more as one people, united by history. The Zionist movement which began in the 19th century greatly influenced the situation.

Diversity within Christianity is just as great but expressed in different ways by the great Christian denominations. The self-understanding of individual Churches is determined by varying intellectual traditions and historical developments, while often originating in a delimitation from Christians of other beliefs. In our century, though, the ecumenical movement has set the Churches on the path to mutual recognition and a realization of the unity of Christians.

In developing an ecumenical community, the Christian Churches cannot evade the question of whether and in what way they are linked to the Jews. Certain statements on the relationship between the Churches and the Jews prove that the former have become aware of this problem. The unique position of Israel as people of the covenant was strongly emphasized already at the First World Conference of Churches in Amsterdam. Many Christians see the continued existence of the Jewish people after the coming of Jesus Christ as an inscrutable mystery which they understand as a sign of the immutable fidelity of God.

2. The Two Modes of Jewish Existence

Since earliest times, Jews have been living in the land of Israel as well as outside of it. Only a part of those deported into Babylonian exile, for instance, returned to the country. Later on, a Jewish diaspora developed in Syria, Egypt, and the whole Mediterranean area, by emigration and missionary work. At the time of Jesus, the diaspora was culturally important and numerically stronger than the Jewry within the country of Israel. In our time, too, the majority of Jews live outside the country.

Jewish faith, nevertheless, inseparably links the election of the people to the election of the land. The Book of Deuteronomy clearly says that only within the country can Israel be fully obedient to God. Her prophets promise the return of the people to the land, where the Torah can be fulfilled and God will establish His Kingdom. Jews have always held fast to this bond between people and land. After the failure of the Jewish wars of liberation in the first and second century AD, Jewish life was at times very precarious and existed in certain parts of the country only, mainly in Galilee. At that time Jewish teachers demanded that the people remain in the country or return there. In their prayers Jews ask every day: "Unite us from the four corners of the earth." The liturgy of the first Passover night culminates in the exclamation: "Next year in Jerusalem." Many details of the Law as well as all festivals of the Jewish year are based on this link between people and land, so that in the traditional view Jewish existence can be fully lived only in the country of Israel.

That makes diaspora life a temporary situation which must be overcome and that is why, diaspora Jews since the times of antiquity have again and again been trying to maintain contact with the land. An individual could achieve such contact by donations for those living in the country, by pilgrimages, or by a return—if only to be buried there. Again and again, immigration by sizeable groups took place, often impelled by messianic movements. The Zionist settlement movement of the last one hundred years is but a link in this long chain of attempts to restore the unity of people and land.

Yet, diaspora life was not merely considered a fate to be endured, an inscrutable divine path, or a temptation to surrender through assimilation. There always existed individual Jews and Jewish groups who saw in the diaspora a chance for the Jewish people to make known among the nations the message of the One God. Religiously, ethically, and culturally, the Jewish diaspora made considerable contributions to many nations. The origin and development of Christianity and Islam were largely stamped by continuous contact with the Jewish diaspora, just as Jews received impulses by living among other nations and religions.

3. The State of Israel

Jewish settlement in the country and the situation after Auschwitz were the two decisive factors leading to the founding of the State.

Toward the end of the 19th century, traditional anti-Judaism among Christians developed into a new form of racist anti-Semitism. In its final consequence, it culminated in the mass murder of European Jewry by the National Socialist state. Following this indescribable catastrophe, the major powers finally gave support and recognition to the demand for an independent state in Palestine. The founding of the state brought to a close the development that, since the end of the 19th century, had made the old land of Israel to an ever increasing degree, a place of refuge for persecuted Jews.

It was not only the pressure of an inimical environment, though, that caused Jews to return to their land but the realization of a longing for Zion, sustained for millenia. Beyond its political function, then, the State of Israel has religious meaning for many Jews: They perceive of the Bible and post-biblical tradition in a completely new manner. More and more, Israel is becoming an intellectual centre that influences the diaspora. A basic Israeli law grants all Jews the privilege to live in the country and obtain citizens' rights, thereby endeavoring to guarantee the survival of diaspora Jews in case of renewed persecutions or threats to their identity.

Politically speaking, Israel is a modern secular state, organized as a parliamentary democracy, just as in antiquity the Jewish people fashioned their state on contemporary models. Yet, such a characterization does not fully describe the modern State: Its name and founding document expressly place it within the tradition of Judaism and, thereby, within the context of the chosen people's history. It is the task of the State of Israel to guarantee the existence of this people in the country of their forefathers. This implication has meaning for Christians as well. After all the injustice inflicted upon the Jews—particularly by Germans—Christians are obligated to recognize and support the internationally valid United Nations Resolution of 1948 which is intended to enable Jews to live a secure life in a state of their own.

At the same time, Christians must energetically work toward the proper settlement of justified claims by both sides, Arabs and Jews. Neither should the Palestinian Arabs alone have to bear the consequences of the conflict, nor should only Israel be held responsible for the situation. For that reason, even those not directly involved, must participate in efforts to procure a durable peace in the Middle East. German Christians in particular must not evade their part in this task. They will also have to strengthen their bond with Arab Christians who by the conflict were placed in a very difficult situation.

4. Jews-Christians-Germans

We Christians pay heed to the particular difficulties arising out of the relationship between Germans and Jews. A long common history of Jews and Christians in Germany has frequently resulted in mutual stimulation as well as antagonism. Ever recurring enmity against Jews is due not only to religious causes but to economic, political, and cultural ones as well. Based on Christian-Germanic and racist ideologies, Jew-hatred in Germany during the 19th and 20th centuries became especially virulent. In its ultimate consequence, it led to the persecutions of Jews after 1933 and, finally, to the murder of about six million Jews in Europe.

Up to the beginning of the Second World War, many German Jews were able to escape, especially through emigration, the fate that threatened them. During the War, however, men, women, and children in Germany and all the occupied countries were deported to extermination camps and murdered. Only a few Jews during that time were still able to emigrate or go into hiding. Together with the Jews, millions of non-Jews became the victims of persecution.

Only a few Germans had full knowledge of the entire plan of destruction but most of them knew of the legislation and public Jew-baiting in 1933, the burning of synagogues and plundering of stores in November 1938, and the sudden disappearance of Jewish neighbors and school fellows. Rumors and foreign news broadcasts also added to the available information. Yet, most Germans did not believe or did not want to believe the planned destruction of European Jewry, the so-called "final solution". They set their mind at rest with the news of a resettlement of Jews in Eastern Europe; the Christian Churches were largely silent. Only a few people who thereby endangered their own life, helped Jews to flee or kept them in hiding.

The extermination of six million Jews and the almost complete destruction of Jewish culture in Europe caused a profound trauma in the mind of the Jewish people all over the world. Its effects, which will make themselves felt for generations to come, often find expression in insecurity and anxiety as well as over-sensitivity toward any endangerment of Jewish existence.

Jews in Israel and the diaspora identify the catastrophe of the holocaust by the name of Auschwitz in Poland, the largest of all the extermination camps. Similar to Hiroschima, Auschwitz became the symbol for the experienced horrors of extermination. It also was a turning point in historical and theological thinking, especially in Judaism.

Out of these culpable omissions of the past, special obligations arise for us Christians in Germany, namely to fight newly developing anti-Semitism, even under the guise of politically and socially motivated anti-Zionism. We must cooperate in a new relationship with Jews.

5. Common Tasks

Today's efforts to re-fashion the relationship between Christians and Jews have made both of them aware again that, despite all contrasts, they hold much in common. It follows that this common ground must be concretely developed in the present and for the future. After all that has happened it behooves us to proceed with great care. Only tentative beginnings can be indicated. The belief that man as the image of God bears responsibility for the whole earth, including the shape of human life, could serve as a point of departure.

People of various religions and beliefs in all continents are fighting for a more humane world and Christians and Jews must take part. Their faith in the One God who created one humanity, challenges them—as well as the Muslims—to stand up for solidarity with all men. Without the conviction that every human being is of equal worth before God, the development of human rights is unthinkable in our time.

In their "General Declaration of Human Rights" of December 10, 1948, the United Nations proclaimed the rights of all men. It is all the more frightening to see how much the reality remains in arrear of this program. That applies to lack of social justice, to discrimination, persecution, and maltreatment for racist, religious, and political reasons.

Holy Scripture, to which Jews and Christians refer their life, emphasizes the love of God for the disadvantaged and deprived. It is a task, then, for Christians and Jews to fight against the power of those who succeed and enrich themselves at the expense of the weak. Another important task, despite all evident difficulties, must be the joint effort of Christians, Jews, and Muslims on behalf of justice and peace in the Middle East.

The ever more apparent threat by technology to human existence makes it imperative to comprehend the world once more as a creation of God, to deal with it appropriately and according to the mandate received from God. That means that we turn away from a position in which man makes himself the measure of all things, exploits the world for his own good exclusively, and thereby becomes dependent on what he himself has produced. It is primarily a question of Christians and Jews becoming aware of their common responsibility for the development of society and its realization, which will result in further areas of joint action.

6. Encounter and Witness

Christians and Jews interpret and confess in different ways their faith in the One God who reveals Himself in history. The Torah, as the centre of Jewish faith, is a divine plan and tool for the development and fulfillment of the world. Jesus Christ takes that place in Christianity, as salvation for all men. In the face of such common ground as well as differences, the encounter between Christians and Jews must not be confined to a mere social meeting. Joint listening to Holy Scripture may lead to an enrichment and clarification of one's own faith. The more open and intensive such an encounter will be, the more candid can we discuss that which separates the two groups.

Yet, both must witness to their own faith: The divine charge makes the believer a witness who by word and deed must realize his identity as Christian or Jew. An encounter on this basis can hope to be fruitful only if the long and painful history of mutual relations is conscientiously taken into account.

To spread the faith among the nations, was a characteristic of Judaism at the time of Jesus. The early Christian community followed along the same path, to fulfil the mission received from its Risen Lord. It resulted in widespread Christian missionary activity among Jews and Gentiles and brought about the formation of communities composed partly of Jews and partly of Gentiles.

At the beginning of the Church, Jews could be baptized in the name of Jesus and continue to belong to the Jewish people. In the course of a divergent development, conversion to Christianity gradually implied a loss of Jewish identity.

With the growing expansion of Christianity, the Jews became a minority. In the end, Judaism became the only religious minority suffered under the aegis of a state church that defined all areas of community life. Under this unequal distribution of power, a great deal of pressure was put on the Jews in the course of centuries. Apart from persecutions and expulsions, forced conversions took place as well as religious discussions which were to prove the superiority of Christianity. The proper meaning of a Christian witness toward Jews was thereby often obscured and turned into its opposite.

Changed intellectual and social conditions in the modern world generated serious attempts among Protestants to regain the original meaning of a Christian witness toward Jews. That applies particularly to the era of a developing Pietism which, by referring back to the Reformation, re-emphasized the freedom of the Gospels. The effects of Christian social superiority were somewhat softened by the personal witness of individual Christians who turned toward the Jews. From such religious motifs developed the mission to the Jews which led to fruitful encounters between Christians and Jews. A renewed Christian interest in Judaism, particularly from a scholarly point of view, was thereby awakened. Since the Enlightenment and due in part only to the mission to the Jews, more and more Jews converted to Christianity for social reasons.

After a period of growing anti-Semitism during the 19th and 20th centuries during which some Christians protected individual Jews and after the terrible events of National Socialist persecution of the Jews, the situation has changed in many ways. The Church has lost much of her former importance in public life and her extensive failure during the Jewish persecutions has again and to a very serious degree shaken her unprejudiced witness toward the Jews.

The witness to our own faith, necessary for a fruitful encounter, has become severely encumbered by shortcomings and faulty elements of Christian customs in the past. Missionary practices exist even today which give Jews justified cause for suspicion. Such practices, however, are decidedly rejected by the Church and even by those individuals who favor a missionary witness toward the Jews. Such misuse, however, does not release Christians from an authentic endeavor to render account according to the Gospels, "for the hope that is in you" (1 Pet 3:15). Faith must not remain silent.

After all that has happened, there are many different opinions on the proper way of Christian witness. The discussion during the last few years has centered mainly on the terms '"mission" and "dialogue"; these were often interpreted as mutually exclusive. We have now come to understand mission and dialogue as two dimensions of one Christian witness and this insight corresponds to the more recent view of Christian mission generally.

Mission and dialogue as descriptions of Christian witness have an ominous sound to Jewish ears. Christians must, therefore, re-assess the meaning with regard to the Jews, of their witness to Jesus Christ as salvation for all mankind, the terms by which to identify their witness, and the methods of procedure.

The Church must not fail to admit and candidly state that she stands in need of talking to the Jews. Such dialogue will transmit experiences with the God of the Bible which could help every Christian to a more profound insight into his own identity. This aspect is of fundamental importance for the continuing encounter between Christians and Jews.

(The study contains an appendix with information on Jews generally; statistics of European Jewry murdered by the National Socialists; Jews in the Federal Republic of Germany; an account of ecumenical discussions on the Church and the Jews; names and addresses of various Christian organizations; some information on Islam; and the meaning of certain terms used in the above position paper.)

III. JOINT PROTESTANT CATHOLIC DOCUMENT

The Faith and Order Study Group on Christian-Jewish relations was convened in the Fall of 1969 under the aegis of the National Council of Churches' Faith and Order Commission with the cooperation of the Secretariat for Catholic-Jewish Relations of the National Conference of Catholic Bishops. In line with its initial decision to work toward the creation of a major new statement on Christian-Jewish relations, the group spent considerable time in study and discussion of the principal issues with which this statement would have to deal. Input was sought and received from Christian, Jewish and Muslim scholars.

The Executive Committee of the Commission on Faith and Order of the National Council of Churches of Christ in the U.S.A. received on May 31, 1973 A STATEMENT TO OUR FELLOW CHRISTIANS based on a study on Israel: People, Land, State, and took the following action: That A STATEMENT TO OUR FELLOW CHRISTIANS be transmitted to the Commission on Faith and Order and to appropriate Christian and Jewish organizations for study and response with the understanding that

1. it does not carry either approval or endorsement by the Commission;
2. it represents a stage in a process leading, it is hoped, to a fuller theological statement;
3. it is the responsibility of the signatories and not a consensus of the religious communities to which they belong.

1. The Church of Christ is rooted in the life of the People Israel. We Christians look upon Abraham as our spiritual ancestor and father of our faith. For us the relationship is not one of physical descent but the inheritance of a faith like that of Abraham whose life was based on his trust in the promises made to him by God (Gen. 15:1-6). The ministry of Jesus and the life of the early Christian community were thoroughly rooted in the Judaism of their day, particularly in the teachings of the Pharisees. The Christian Church is still sustained by the living faith of the patriarchs and prophets, kings and priests, scribes and rabbis, and the people whom God chose for his own. Christ is the link (Gal. 3:26-29) enabling the Gentiles to be numbered among Abraham's "offspring" and therefore fellow-heirs with the Jews according to God's promise. It is a tragedy of history that Jesus, our

bond of unity with the Jews, has all too often become a symbol and source of division and bitterness because of human weakness and pride.

2.   Christians can also enrich themselves by a careful study of post-biblical Judaism to the present day. Such enrichment is especially imperative in light of the far-reaching value crisis that now affects the entire Western world. If religion is to play its rightful role in the value reconstruction that is now beginning, its approach will have to be ecumenical. And in the West this means, first of all, the recognition that two religious traditions, not a single Judaeo-Christian tradition, have shaped our culture; and secondly, the genuine and open sharing of insights and differences between Jews and Christians, each realizing that one's understanding of the spiritual nature of the human person remains incomplete without the other.

3.   The singular grace of Jesus Christ does not abrogate the covenantal relationship of God with Israel (Rom. 11:1-2). In Christ the Church shares in Israel's election without superseding it. By baptism and faith the Christian, as the Roman liturgy says, passes over to the sonship of Abraham and shares in the dignity of Israel. The survival of the Jewish people, despite the barbaric persecutions and the cruel circumstances under which they were forced to live, is a sign of God's continuing fidelity to the people dear to him. For our spiritual legacy and for all that the Jews have done for the whole human race we Christians are grateful to God and to the people whom God has chosen as a special instrument of his kindness.

4.   The new ecumenical atmosphere in theological research and the tragic reality of the Holocaust together with the present Middle East conflict urge us to reconsider the relationship of Christians to Jews. We Christians have already acknowledged that God made a covenant with the Jews in the past, promising his paternal care for his chosen people in return for their fidelity. Unfortunately many Christians have assumed that the validity of Judaism ended with the beginning of Christianity, the rejection of Jesus as Messiah marking the dissolution of the covenant. This assumption conflicts sharply with St. Paul's declaration that God did not annul his promise to the chosen people since God never takes back his gifts or revokes his call (Rom. 11, 28-29). The Apostle dismissed as altogether untenable the notion that God has rejected his people.
There is thus strong Scriptural support for the position that God's covenant love for the Jewish people remains firm. The continuity of contemporary Judaism with ancient Israel demonstrates the abiding validity of Jewish worship and life as authentic forms of service to the true God.

5.   The fierce persecution of Jews by Christians through the centuries should be seen as a fratricidal strife as well as a vast human tragedy. In many instances Christian preachers and writers disseminated slanderous stories about the Jews. From the apostolic age the Church accepted uncritically the condemnation of the Pharisees as hypocrites even though the Synoptic Gospels picture Jesus as generally agreeing with what many

Pharisees actually stood for. Whole generations of Christians looked with contempt upon this people who were condemned to remain wanderers on the earth on the charge, in fact false, of having killed Christ. Anti-Jewish polemics became a perennial feature of Christendom and reflected gross ignorance of Jewish history and religion. This sin has infected the non-Christian world as well.

6. A major source of friction in contemporary Christian-Jewish relations is Christian hostility and indifference to the State of Israel. In dialogue among Christians on the Middle East question there exists a startling variety of opinions, some of which exacerbate already existing Christian-Jewish misunderstandings. We urge the churches therefore to give their prayerful attention to such central questions as the legitimacy of the Jewish state, the rights of the Palestinians, and the problem of the refugees — Jewish as well as Arab. Only a conscience seeking to be well-informed and free of prejudice can help to bring about peace with justice in the Middle East.

7. The validity of the State of Israel rests on moral and juridical grounds. It was established in response to a resolution of the U.N. General Assembly, after termination of the British Mandate. However, involved in the potentially explosive political conflict in the Middle East is a theological question that demands careful scrutiny. What is the relationship between "the people" and "the land"? What is the relation between the chosen people and the territory comprising the present State of Israel? There is no Christian consensus on these questions. Genesis explicitly affirms a connection between the people and the land (Gen. 15:18), and even within the New Testament certain passages imply such a connection. Therefore, Christians who see Israel as something more than a political state are not wrongly theologizing politics by understanding the existence of the Jewish state in theological terms. They are merely recognizing that modern Israel is the homeland of a people whose political identity is sustained by the faith that God has blessed them with a covenant. There is reason for Christians to rejoice that the Jewish people are no longer required to live in enforced dispersion among the nations, separated from the land of the promise.

8. We have traditionally viewed the Jews as a people having a universal dimension. God wanted them to set up a special society dedicated to the fulfillment of the messianic aspirations for righteousness and freedom. Even when dispersed they became a summons to the human conscience to safeguard and protect the rights of all people. Here in the United States the Jewish contribution to the advancement of human rights remains outstanding. Now the question arises: is the Jewish people so universalistic as to exclude the possibility of their having a state of their own? It does seem to many observers that the localizing of Jewish activities gives a greater opportunity to fulfill their universal vocation than would an unfocused global presence.

9.   As a political state, Israel is open to all the temptations of power. As a result of its military triumphs in the Six-Day War, the charge is sometimes made that Israel is belligerently expansionistic. Visitors to Israel, however, can easily discover that the overriding concern of the majority of Israelis is peace, not more territory. Israel's anxiety about national defense reflects the age-old human yearning for security, the anxiety of a people whose history has been a saga of frightful persecution, climaxed by the Holocaust of six million men, women and children. Against such a tormented background, is it surprising that the Jewish people should want to defend themselves? It would be quite unrealistic and unjust to expect Israel to become a sort of heavenly society of which more is demanded than of other nations. This does not mean that Christians must endorse every policy decision by the Israeli government. Many Jews, both within Israel and without, do not do so. Rather, Christians must refrain from the type of criticism that would use Israel's failures, real or imagined, to live up to the highest moral standards as an excuse to deny its right to exist. Such a view would be a double standard, one not applied to any other nation on earth.

10.   As Christians we urge all nations in the world (our own nation, Israel, and the Arab states included) to recognize that there is no way to secure lasting peace based on the balance of military power and the use of fear as a deterrent. Rather, the only road leading to peace is trust in and understanding of neighbors and partners. We urge the Church to attend to its role as an agent of reconciliation.

11.   At present antisemitism is unfashionable and seems to have gone underground in the United States, though some recent studies show it is on the rise. But even an underground antisemitism surfaces from time to time in various forms and disguises. New Left literature has excoriated the Jews not as Jews but as "Zionists." Antisemitism, however, is a difficult virus to counteract. It has a pervasiveness that infects our whole civilization and manifests itself in education, housing, job opportunities and social life. Fortunately some Christian churches are working hard to excise from their liturgy and education any antisemitic references.

12.   Those who refuse to learn from history must relive the errors and evils of the past. In times of civil disorders, agitators have arisen and will continue to appear in our society attempting to make Jews the scapegoats for the evils of an era. If problems like inflation and unemployment continue to escalate, if a depression should set in, we can be fairly sure that the radical Right and/or the radical Left will make Jews out to be the culprits.

13.   The pressure of our violent times urges us as Christians to live up to our calling as ministers of reconciliation, ready and willing to stifle rumors about the Jews and to build up an atmosphere of brotherly understanding in Christian-Jewish relations. We strongly commend Jewish-Christian dialogue as a favored instrument by which we may explore the richness of Judaism and the Jewish roots of our Christian faith.

14. The pain of the past has taught us that antisemitism is a Pandora's box from which spring out not only atrocities against Jews but also contempt for Christ. Whatever the antisemite inflicts on the Jews he inflicts on Christ who is "bone of their bone and flesh of their flesh." In the words of St. Paul, "They are Israelites and to them belong the sonship, the glory, the covenants, the giving of the law, the worship and the promises; to them belong the partriarchs, and of their race according to the flesh is the Christ" (Rom. 9:4-5).

(These recommendations and the following questions for further study are attached to the Faith and Order Document).

We call upon Christians to recognize and to respond to God's love for the Jewish people. We affirm this love to be expressed by his presence with them in history to this day and by his choice of them as bearers of the Christ, His Son. We perceive this love to require concrete responses in the life and work of the Christian churches. Among such responses we recommend the following:

1. Sensitivity and balance in use of New Testament texts
There are numerous NT texts which might be interpreted as reflecting negatively on Jews and Judaism. In reading and interpreting such texts we must constantly remember that Jesus was a Jew. His forebears were Jews. He lived and taught among the Jews. His dress, his manner of speaking, his mode of life, his teaching reflected the Judaism of the time. Therefore, conflict and controversies must be seen as taking place within a framework which he not only shared with fellow-Jews, but which he and God affirmed.

Caution in this respect is particularly advisable when treating the Pharisees. Conflicts with the Pharisees were internal Jewish struggles. The diatribes reflect serious family quarrels which took place between Jews and Jesus' followers in the nascent church. They underline God's choice to reveal himself through a Jewish context, rather than indicating a total rejection of Jews or Pharisees. Jesus, in fact, agreed with Pharisaic perspectives on many points, as did Paul and other early church leaders.

2. Preaching which portrays or refers to Jews, Judaism and the OT in a positive light
Christian preaching employs negative as well as positive examples, images, and experimental analogies. We try to teach what not to do as well as what to do. Some examples of what not to do lie ready at hand in the words or actions of Jews in the NT. Preachers must guard against any tendency to

portray Jews or Jewish groups as negative models. The truth and beauty of Christianity should not be enhanced by setting up Jews or Judaism as false and ugly. Likewise the OT witness should not be portrayed as less authoritative, less normative, or superseded. It is central to the tradition which our Lord accepted as his own and which he reaffirmed as He interpreted it in his life, work, and thought. The Judgment and the redeeming love of God should be presented as existing from the beginning to the end of both Testaments.

3. Receptivity to the way in which God's love continues to be revealed in Jewish self-expression
The varieties of modern Jewish religious and social experience reaffirm God's mysterious loving purpose in our world today. Fulfillment of commandments and ordinances, liturgy, festivals, family life, communal experience, the State of Israel, and many other aspects of Jewish experience inspire, influence, edify and challenge us. Christians must confront and respond with warmth and openness to the ways in which God is speaking and acting in and through Jewish life today.

As a corollary, we must prepare to speak and act forthrightly against all efforts to distort or to negate the status or value of Jewish life and experience. Jews are pilgrims with us, recipients of God's gracious love, sojourners on the way to salvation.

Questions for Further Study

1. In what sense are Christians "God's chosen people"? Is this an exclusive claim, or is the Jewish people part of God's continuing work in history (Romans 9:4)? If "chosen," what are Christians "chosen" for?

2. In what sense are the Jews a covenant people? Are Christians possessors of a second covenant, a shared covenant, or a renewed covenant?

3. Is an ecumenical movement without the Jewish component dependable and valid? What is the role of Christian-Jewish dialogue in the future of the church? What are the agreed areas of Jewish-Christian cooperation?

4. What is the meaning of the Holocaust to believing Christians? What is the responsibility of Christendom in relation to the Holocaust?

5. Is not antisemitism a betrayal of the faith? Is not antisemitism also antichristianity (Heschel)?

6. To what extent must Jews and Christians read the Jewish scriptures (which we call "Old Testament") differently?

a) Does the acceptance of Jesus Christ mean reading the OT differently?

b) In what sense are certain events in Jewish history — like the Exodus and Sinai — also formative for the Christian faith?

7. How can Christianity benefit from post-biblical Judaism?

8. To what extent have Christians taught and are still teaching that which creates religious antisemitism and lays the foundations for the political antisemitism whose horrors we have seen in recent decades?

9. Should there be a conversionist mission to the Jews in the light of Paul's statements (Rom 9)?

10. Does the land of Israel have a special meaning for Christians? Is this meaning merely figurative?

11. Compare the concept of the Messiah in Christianity and Judaism.

a) What does it mean to say Jesus Christ is "the Messiah" (a Jewish word)?

b) Do we share in the Jewish anticipation of the Messianic era?

c) What are the implications for Christians that the Messianic era does not appear to have come?